# The Parenting Puzzle

# The Parenting Puzzle: Your Guide to Transforming Family Life

THE CENTRE FOR
**EMOTIONAL**
**HEALTH**

First published in the United Kingdom in 2003 by

The Centre for Emotional Health
Units 2 & 3 Fenchurch Court
Bobby Fryer Close
Oxford OX4 6ZN

www.centreforemotionalhealth.org.uk

The Centre for Emotional Health is a registered charity 1062514.

A CIP catalogue record for this book is available
from the British Library.

ISBN 978-0-9544709-4-4

Written by Candida Hunt and Annette Mountford MBE

Cartoons by Val Saunders

Design by Cat Davis - madebycat.co.uk (adapted from original design by Joanna Turner)

Printed in the UK

The Centre for Emotional Health is a national charity dedicated to creating an emotionally healthy, resilient and responsible society.

The Parenting Puzzle is designed for use by parents and carers and by those who support them. It does not qualify facilitators to lead Nurturing Programme parenting groups. If you are interested in becoming a Parent Group Leader, please contact us about our training courses.

# The Parenting Puzzle

The Four constructs

The Question of Discipline

Kinds of Touch

Feelings... and how we deal with them

Giving Praise

Choices and Consequences

Continuing the Family Journey

Rewards and Penalties

Communicating Clearly: "I" Statements

Family Rules

Personal Power and Self-esteem

Problem Solving and Negotiating

Helping Children Grow Up

Time to Calm Down

Ages and stages

Keeping Children Safe

Behaviour to Ignore

Nurturing Ourselves

Parenting Styles

# Contents

# Before We Begin

Welcome to *The Parenting Puzzle* and thank you for taking the time to explore this book and find out what it offers to parents and all those who work with families. Families come in all shapes and sizes, they have their own unique family culture, but there are two key messages that we nearly always hear: that parents and carers want to give their children the very best chance in life and that sometimes being a parent or carer can be the toughest job there is. This is where The Centre for Emotional Health and *The Parenting Puzzle* are here to help. The Centre for Emotional Health is a national charity dedicated to creating an emotionally healthy, resilient and responsible society.

You may be using this book alongside the sessions of a *Nurturing Programme* Parent Group, or perhaps it's been recommended to you or you came across it when looking for some different parenting ideas. Either way, we hope you find the book accessible, enjoyable and packed full of ideas and strategies to allow everyone in your family to aspire, flourish and achieve.

The Nurturing Programme helps families to flourish

# About the Book

Parenting is one of the most challenging, demanding jobs there is. It can also be one of the most rewarding – though it doesn't always feel like that! We believe that the ideas in *The Parenting Puzzle* can help to make the job easier and more fun much of the time, and more survivable when the going gets tough.

## Background

*The Nurturing Programme*, on which the book is based, was created in the 1970s by Dr Stephen Bavolek out of his work with adolescents and their families. Since then hundreds of thousands of American and UK families have benefited from the programme. It encourages all parents to be confident and positive, and boosts emotional and mental wellbeing in adults and children alike. As parents and carers, we all know that families are not always happy and calm. Living together can be frustrating, difficult and hard work.

## Who is it for?

This is the course workbook for parents and carers who come to the weekly *Nurturing Programme* sessions. It is also a stand-alone self-help book for parents and carers to work through – either on your own or with a friend, a partner or a professional. It gives ideas and activities for family support workers and others supporting families.

## What is it about?

We have designed the book to give, as far as possible, a flavour of the 10 *Nurturing Programme* Parent Group sessions. *The Nurturing Programme* is a tried and tested programme that helps anyone involved in bringing up children to think about what we do, why we do it, and how we feel about it. There is a parallel programme for schools and through the weekly Circle Time sessions in school, children learn to ask themselves the same questions.

## Why is the book needed?

Many of us would like to feel more confident that we're getting our children and teenagers off to a good start in life. This book makes *The Nurturing Programme* available to everyone, not just to those who can join a group.

# HOW is the book organised?

The book is divided into 10 sessions that match the 10 weekly group sessions. Each session starts with some examples of the feedback parents bring to groups about the new things they are trying out at home, and ends with some reflections on the topics covered in the session. Let's get started!

*Within each session there are different activities, some to think about and some to do. To help you, we have used these signs:*

**key message for a major new topic**

**stop and think and answer the question by yourself**

**if there is space make a note of your ideas**

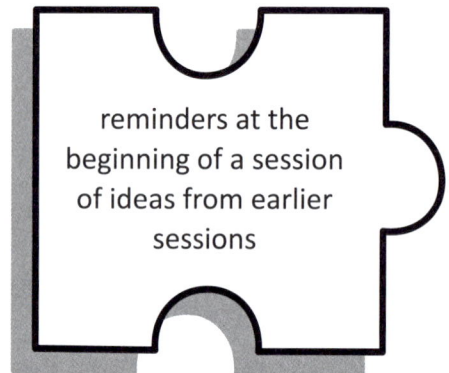

reminders at the beginning of a session of ideas from earlier sessions

## charts for activities to do for yourself

fill in as a reminder of an activity done in a group; there are completed charts to check against as well

**have a go at doing an activity, or writing down your ideas**

.................................................

.................................................

.................................................

## STEPS

**1** recommended steps to follow when trying out

**2** a new idea at home

## Practice sheets

to help you try something out before doing it for real with the family

.................................................

**examples of questions and comments from parents**

Throughout the book there are speech bubbles which represent parents' or carers' thoughts or comments as they have discussed or learnt about the same things. They can be useful examples to relate to or to give another perspective.

*Here is an example of a cartoon to give you an idea*

We have included cartoons all the way through the book as examples of how to go about putting ideas into practice (and sometimes how not to, as well!).

SAT SUN MON TUES WED THURS FRI SAT SUN

Time to have a go

Put it into practice!

FRI THURS WED

MON TUES WED

WED SAT FRI THURS WED TUES MON SUN

At the end of the session there are suggestions about what to do, either between the weekly group sessions, or before reading the next session. Talking, reading and thinking about the Programme is great; putting it into practice is even more important!

Some weeks family life may be fairly calm, and you'll find time and energy to try something new; at other times keeping our heads above water is the best we can manage. It's fine if you don't do everything at first – you can always come back to it. You may feel like trying out all the ideas, or may find it easier to try one or two things at a time, and get comfortable with those before moving on to something else.

Sometimes we notice that we're responding in a different way just as a result of having thought about what's going on. Do whatever suits you best. One thing is certain: if we stay the same, nothing around us is likely to change.

# other Resources

There are other ways in which you can access the information in this book. The Centre for Emotional Health's website contains free downloads for you to use including: Top Tips, Practise Sheets, Ideas for Activities to do with your Children, Kindness Charts and Information on Internet Safety. If you are using this book independently and would like to find a parent group there's also information that may help you to do this.

## www.centreforemotionalhealth.org.uk/parent-zone

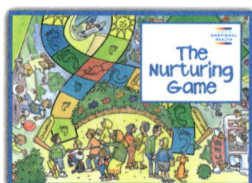

The Nurturing Game is a board game which provides a great opportunity for players to talk, listen and learn more about themselves and others. Players follow a path through the park and on the way they pick cards that encourage them to think about their feelings, self-awareness and the choices they make.

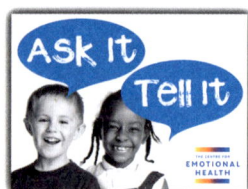

Ask It Tell It is a simple game that encourages families to listen to one another's thoughts and feelings by asking simple questions, e.g. "What is something that makes you happy?" or "A funny thing that happened to me was…."

Both games are great conversation starters and fun to play with children from about 3 years.

If you're the parent of a teenager, you may also find the Talking Teens booklet helpful. Packed with practical ideas to help improve relationships with teenagers, the booklet offers an opportunity to understand something of what's going on in the adolescent brain and provides strategies for supporting and communicating with young people.

These resources are available from:

## shop.familylinks.org.uk/shop

# we'd like to thank...

## Stephen J. Bavolek PhD

the creator of
The Nurturing Programme on which
The Parenting Puzzle is based

## Annette Mountford

for her extraordinary passion
and commitment to The Nurturing
Programme, and for bringing the
programme to so many practitioners and
parents across the UK

## Candida Hunt

for her writing and editorial skills,
and for sharing her wisdom having
led so many Nurturing Programme
parenting groups

## Rosalind Portman

for her ongoing support,
encouragement and enthusiasm for
The Centre for Emotional Health
and The Nurturing Programme

## practitioners and parents across the UK

who have helped shape and inform
this book over the years

# Session 1: Building Blocks: The Four Constructs and Giving Praise

# Departure Point

Becoming a parent is a bit like starting on a journey. We might have an idea about where we want to go, how we want to travel, what we'd like to enjoy along the way – or we might not be clear about these things. We may feel excited and curious, or anxious, or reluctant. We may or may not feel confident about what it will be like and how we will manage.

Journeys often turn out to be different from what we expected. And most long journeys have different stages, some of which we find easier and more enjoyable than others. Sometimes everything goes smoothly. Sometimes there are challenges that we cope with really well. We can also have accidents and disasters, and wonder why we decided to go on the journey in the first place. All this is true of being a parent and raising a family, too.

Let's pause so you can think about where you are on your family's journey, and how it feels; and also what your aims are as a parent. If you'd like to, write down your ideas in the thought bubbles on the next page. (When you get to the end of the book, there'll be a chance to do this again – and it can be interesting to compare your "before" and "after" thoughts.)

*Here are some questions to help you think about it. You don't have to answer these – your own ideas and thoughts are the important ones.*

## How we are getting on as a family

- **?** **Do we have fun together – at all, at home, when we're out?**
- **?** **Do we fight a lot, or get on well most of the time?**
- **?** **Do I have to nag or shout before anyone does what I ask?**
- **?** **Am I enjoying being a parent, or is it exhausting and stressful?**

## My aims/hopes/goals as a parent

- **?** **What are my immediate aims?**
- **?** **What do I hope for us as a family?**
- **?** **What kind of relationship would I like to have with my children when they are grown up?**

## How we are getting on as a family

...............................................................................................

...............................................................................................

...............................................................................................

...............................................................................................

...............................................................................................

...............................................................................................

## My aims/hopes/goals as a parent

...............................................................................................

...............................................................................................

...............................................................................................

...............................................................................................

...............................................................................................

...............................................................................................

...............................................................................................

# Building Blocks: The Four Constructs

The Nurturing Programme is based on four ideas, called the Four Constructs. These provide the building blocks for positive, constructive relationships and confident parenting. They support good emotional health for parents and children.

Being emotionally healthy involves being aware of our own feelings, being able to find safe ways to express and manage feelings, and being sensitive to the feelings of others. Having good emotional health helps us and our children to interact socially with others, cope with stress and participate fully in family and school or work life.

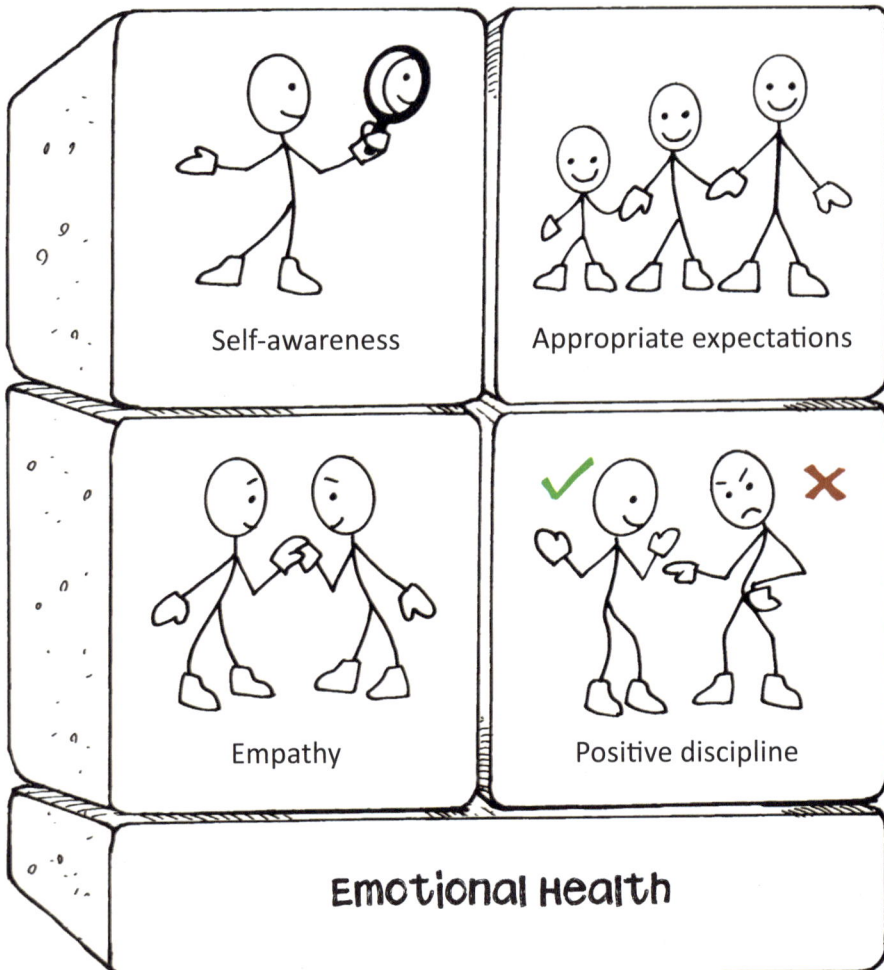

Self-awareness

Appropriate expectations

Empathy

Positive discipline

Emotional Health

# Self-awareness

The art of self-awareness is to know ourselves well – what we do and don't like, what our needs are, how we feel. If we are sensitive towards ourselves, it's easier to look after our needs and have the physical and emotional energy to care for others.

Understanding the effects of what happened to us when we were children helps us to make choices in our relationships with our own children.

# Appropriate expectations

Children grow up in different ways: physically, intellectually, socially and emotionally. We need to match our expectations to what they can actually do. They learn all the thousands of skills at different rates. What one child finds easy  another child of the same age might find hard. If we expect too much or too little of them, children tend to become rebellious, frustrated and angry, or give up in despair. It is helpful to them if we recognise each small step in their learning.

# Empathy

Empathy means tuning in to someone else's feelings, understanding their emotional point of view. It is the cornerstone of The Nurturing Programme. We don't have to agree with what the other person thinks – just to be sensitive to the way they feel, and to accept it. An empathic response to children's moods makes our relationship with them happier and closer. Children who are treated with empathy and respect will learn to be empathic and respectful towards other people.

*It's so disappointing that Tom's ill and can't come to play. I'm not surprised you're upset. Would you like to draw him a picture to help him get better quickly?*

*Your tower looks great! I can see you're feeling proud to have built such a tall one.*

# Positive discipline

There's no doubt that children need discipline to learn what behaviour is OK and what is not. Positive discipline focuses on praise, rewards, giving choices, negotiating and responsibility. There are also fair penalties for poor behaviour. It makes life more enjoyable for parents and for children, and helps to build self-esteem in the family.

Negative discipline uses punishment and fear; it is stressful for everyone.

*Thank you for helping to put away the shopping. Here's a sticker to add to our kindness chart.*

*We agreed you would tidy up the DVDs by teatime and you haven't done it. No more TV for you today.*

# Using Empathy

Empathy is so important that we'll look at it some more. Here's an example of a situation that could be handled in an unhelpful, negative way or an empathic, helpful way.

## 🙁 Unempathic (unhelpful)

## 🙂 Empathic (helpful)

**Can you think of a situation where someone failed to respect your feelings? How did you feel towards that person?**

**Can you also think of a time when someone responded empathically to you, really tuning in to your feelings? And how did you feel towards them?**

If we notice how helpful it can be when someone truly accepts the way we feel, we're more likely to try to tune in to other people's feelings, too.

# Steps for Empathy

**1**   Stop what you are doing

**2**   Give full attention and listen

**3**   Give appropriate eye contact/body language and facial expressions

**4**   Try and find the feelings behind the words

**5**   Tentatively suggest the feeling behind the words

Empathic phrases may start like this: *"I'm wondering..."*

*"You seem..."*   *"It sounds as though..."*   *"You sound/look like..."*

*"It can be hard when...."*   *"I can hear..."*   *"I can see..."*

**6**   Allow them time to tell their story if they want to, or walk away/be silent as they wish

**7**   Do avoid questioning, commanding, advice, or instructions

**8**   Do use gentle touch if appropriate

**9**   Keep focused on the person's feelings

**10**   Avoid fixing it or over-reacting

# Giving Praise

**Praise is the magic ingredient in relationships. It's a powerful way of encouraging and supporting other people, of showing that we are pleased, enthusiastic or grateful. It helps children and adults, including ourselves, to feel good.**

With children, praise works wonders. They need to know when we like what they are doing; it isn't enough just to tell them when we don't like the way they behave. They respond better to compliments than to criticism, nagging or shouting. The glow of pleasure and pride they feel when their efforts are noticed helps them to remember what is wanted, and to try again another time.

Some people find saying nice things to others awkward or difficult, and feel embarrassed when someone pays them a compliment or congratulates them for having done something well. Criticism seems to come more easily – because it's more familiar. The more we practise giving and receiving praise, the easier it becomes.

**Won't the kids get big-headed if I praise them?**

**"No, not if the praise is deserved and genuine, and if it is balanced by clear boundaries and fair penalties when they choose to behave badly."**

**Why should I praise my children?**

**"Praise helps children to remember what we'd like them to do, how we expect them to behave. Praise helps us to notice all the good things about our children, rather than mostly focusing on their faults."**

**It's a tough world. Isn't it better to prepare kids for that by not making them soft with praise or dependent on it?**

**"It's helpful to learn to give and receive praise comfortably – it helps us survive life's difficulties rather than adding to them."**

# Giving Praise Effectively

Here are two ways of praising - Unhelpful and Effective. See how many differences you can spot in the parent's responses to the child.

## ☹ Unhelpful praise

*Look Dad, I got a star for my picture at school. My teacher said it was really good. It's my best one ever!*

*Oh yes, well done. It's brilliant. You're a good girl.*

*But Dad, you're not looking. I want to show it to you.*

*I've told you it's a very nice picture. Now leave me in peace.*

*He doesn't care. I feel like throwing the stupid picture away.*

## ☺ Effective praise

*Look Dad, I got a star for my picture at school. My teacher said it was really good. It's my best one ever!*

*How exciting! Let me see. What great colours you've chosen. What do you like best?*

*I like the clouds because they look quite real.*

*I like them too. You deserve to feel proud of yourself for drawing and colouring so well.*

*I like making pictures. I think I'll do another one later.*

If you are already giving praise, you may like to check how you are doing it and see if you want to change or add anything. If the idea is new, you could start with just one or two of these ideas, and use more of them as you get used to giving praise. Thinking about what you could praise, and rehearsing in your mind what you'd like to say, makes it easier at first.

# Steps for Giving Praise Effectively

1. Give the child all your attention

2. Move close to the child

3. Look pleased and share their pleasure

4. Be specific: describe what you like

5. Ask the child what he/she thinks

6. Seek eye contact

7. Mean it - be sincere and let it show in a warm tone of voice.

8. Touch the child gently

9. Give pride to the child (*"You deserve to feel proud of yourself"*)

# Praise for Being and Praise for Doing

We want children to feel good about themselves. When they feel good they are more likely to behave well. We want to feel good about ourselves too.

For children and adults this feeling of self worth grows when two needs are met:

I can't think of anything to praise my children for. They behave so badly nearly all the time.

- We need to feel valued and appreciated for who we are

- We also need to feel competent, to believe that we can do things

So all of us need Praise for Being as well as Praise for Doing

## Praise for being

tells someone that we value them just for being who they are – their own qualities, personality, etc. They don't have to do anything to earn the praise; it's unconditional.

## Praise for doing

tells someone that you have noticed what they are doing, and that you like it. If we acknowledge children's efforts, they are more likely to have another go – and more likely to succeed.

Think about your children. If there is one child you find more difficult to praise, it might be a good idea to think particularly about them.

- **?** What could you say, or do, to show that you appreciate and value them for who they are?

- **?** What could you notice and appreciate about what they do well, or are trying to do well?

# Examples of Praise for Being and Praise for Doing

## Praise for Being

I really enjoyed spending time with you today

I'm happy to see you

You're fun to be with

I like your sense of humour

Your bright smile cheers me up

You're very kind to your brothers and sisters

## Praise for Doing

Thank you for helping me put away the shopping

It's great that you're ready on time!

That was a funny joke you told

Well done for tidying your toys away so neatly

You've been working really hard at that

You were very kind to share your toys with your sister

**Add some suggestions for your own children:**

..................................................            ..................................................

..................................................            ..................................................

..................................................            ..................................................

We may well want our children to show particular qualities: to be kind, or sensible, or artistic, or clever. It's good to notice when they are showing these qualities, but try to avoid labelling children, even with apparently positive descriptions.

**?** **What is likely to happen if a particular child is always the 'sensible' or the 'calm' one?**

**?** **How might this limit them?**

**?** **What effect might it have on their relationships with other children?**

Try to notice and appreciate a range of qualities in your children.

# Ways We Can Praise and Encourage Children

Sometimes it can be hard to find the right words. Sometimes it can be hard for children to hear the words too. They may feel embarrassed, or undeserving. We can encourage them just as effectively by gestures and actions, showing that we appreciate them or that we've noticed what they are doing, or trying to do, well.

**Here are some examples of what we might do...**

give a pat on the head/back

put an arm around the child's shoulder

give a thumbs up/high five

display pictures, certificates

clap our hands

smile

give stickers, badges, stars

send a text

award treats and privileges, e.g. choosing an extra game, watching a film together, having a friend to play, going on a special outing, extra pocket money

spending time sharing their interests, and introducing them to our own

**Choose from the list, and add your own ideas too.**
**You're the one who knows your children and what they will enjoy.**

.................................................   .................................................

.................................................   .................................................

.................................................   .................................................

.................................................   .................................................

.................................................   .................................................

.................................................   .................................................

.................................................   .................................................

# Praise Pitfalls

☹ **Unhelpful**   🙂 **Helpful**

> You've got your room so tidy, everything neat and in the right place. Mum really loves you for that.
>
> *When she finds out the drawers are in a mess, she might not love me any more.*

> You've got your room so tidy, everything neat and in the right place. I like the way you've sorted out the cars on the shelf from the bricks in the box – well done.
>
> *Maybe I'll sort out my clothes in the drawers, too.*

It's fine to tell children that we like their behaviour, but they do need our love for them not to have any strings attached – to be unconditional. There are other pitfalls, too: taking the credit, implying criticism, offering advice.

☹ **Unhelpful**   🙂 **Helpful**

> You've been chosen for the team? I knew that making you practise with me would do the trick!

> You've been chosen for the team? Good for you – you deserve it after all the practice you've put in.

☹ **Unhelpful**   🙂 **Helpful**

> Your report is much better this term. You must have started working at last – and about time too.

> Your report is much better this term. Congratulations – I've noticed that you have been working hard, and your teacher says so too.

# Helping Children to Praise

If children hear us giving praise, they will copy us and will learn how to say what they like in other people. We can also encourage children to pat themselves on the back when they have done something well, and to think about how they feel about it.

*Thanks for helping me when I fell over. It was kind of you to help me – you're a good friend.*

*That was a fantastic save – we won the match thanks to you!*

*Thanks for spending so long helping me with my chemistry. I understand it much better now.*

*Getting all your toys sorted was a big job. I hope you're glad it's done – and pleased that it's so much easier to find what you want to play with.*

*It took a lot of courage to keep your hand still while the stitches were put in. You deserve to feel proud of yourself for being so brave.*

*You've been very patient learning to ride your bike –it's not easy getting the hang of it. How do you feel about being able to ride it so well now?*

# Praising ourselves

Many people think the idea of praising themselves is strange – though we're usually quite good at criticising ourselves! It may be hard to think and say kind things about ourselves if nobody else does. We may have grown up thinking we don't deserve any praise – which isn't true. It's never too late to start giving ourselves pats on the back.

Another difficulty is our confusion about the difference between self-praise and being boastful or conceited. Self-praise recognises that we have done something well (praise for doing) or that we have qualities that we value (praise for being). It's boastful only if we make extravagant claims or compare our performance to make us feel superior, "more than" someone else, and them inferior, "less than" us.

### Boasting

*I've cooked a nice supper tonight. It's just as well one of us can cook properly.*

### Self-praise

*I've cooked a nice supper tonight. This is delicious.*

### Boasting

*I scored 52 runs in the match. I played much better than Mark – he was out after only 17 runs.*

### Self-praise

*I scored 52 runs in the match. I was pleased with the way I played today.*

Praising ourselves – out loud sometimes, and quietly to ourselves often, is fine – we deserve it. Praising ourselves in front of children shows them that it's OK for them to pat themselves on the back when they've done well. They will still value praise from others, but they won't be so dependent on other people's approval.

# R E F L E C T I O N S

Being in the group is more fun than I'd thought it might be, and I like listening to everyone's ideas. None of us thinks we've got all the answers!

I'm going to think about those four construct ideas. They sound like a good place to start.

I don't remember being encouraged or praised much when I was a child. I wonder if I can learn to do it - won't they just laugh at me?

The word empathy is new, but I have a friend who's good at it. She never tells me what to do, she just listens to what's going on for me - and it's great!

Here we are at the end of the first session. I hope you've enjoyed it. We've touched on quite a few ideas, and we'll come back to them in later sessions, so don't worry if it doesn't all make sense to you at this stage. It's possible that some of what we've looked at might even feel a bit uncomfortable; if we're not used to giving or getting praise, for example, it can feel strange and artificial at first. It gets easier with practice!

I'd never really thought about the way I'm raising my children. I'm beginning to see that there's more to it than I'd realised.

The important thing is that we're all thinking about how we are bringing up our children, and what we hope for them and for ourselves. We all want the best for our children – if we didn't we wouldn't be here – but it's often not easy to know what will help them when we're caught up in the constant day-to-day busy-ness of being a parent. The Programme gives us the chance to reflect, as well as to explore new ideas together.

# REFLECTIONS

**?** **What are you thinking and feeling at the end of the first session?**
**If you would like to, record your own ideas here.**

........................................................................................

........................................................................................

........................................................................................

........................................................................................

# Time to Have a Go

SUN  MON  TUES  WED  THURS  FRI  SAT  SUN  MON  TUES  WED  THURS  FRI  SAT

Praise everyone in the family at least once, for being and doing.

If you already give quite a lot of praise, notice what kind of praise you give, and how you give it. Does one child get more recognition than another? How about any other adults in the house - we need it too.

Think about the Four Constructs, and how they might be helpful to you as a parent and as a person. They apply to the way we treat ourselves and how we respond to other people.

# Session 2: The Question of Discipline and Time to Calm Down

empathy helps
people to feel
understood

praise
is magic

# What Parents Tell Us

In the groups, there's time at the start of each session for everyone to say what they have tried at home and how it went. As parents we learn a lot from each other, so we will include some of their ideas and suggestions here.

*"My kids thought I'd flipped when I went home and started praising them. I felt quite sad about that - so even though it's hard I'm really trying to give them more."*

*"Yesterday my son thanked me for making his tea. He's never done that before, so I think it must be working in reverse."*

*"I've realised that I find it much easier to be nice to my son than my daughter, so I've been trying hard to notice good things about her too."*

*"There's a lot to take in. I guess it will make more sense by the end of the Programme."*

**?** **As you move through the Programme, you may find it rewarding to chart your progress. Things may get better or sometimes may seem worse, or change may come only slowly – don't worry, this often happens. In the thinks bubble, make a note of how you're getting on if you'd like to.**

I had a go at...

and the result was...

# praise and criticism

**In the first session we thought about praise – why and how to praise. Before we move on, let's think about how we feel when we are praised, and also how we feel when the opposite happens – when we are criticised.**

### ? How do you feel?

If you're not sure, think of a time when someone said something to you that was critical, and stop to notice what feelings arise in you. You may notice just one or two feelings, or many different ones. Then think of another situation, and check again. Some people find they usually react in the same way, and others say the feelings vary depending on the situation and who the other person is (maybe a child, a friend, a parent, the boss, etc.).

Then ask yourself how you feel when someone has praised or encouraged you. Again, to get in touch with your feelings it may help to think of a real situation. If you can't think of one, just ask yourself how you might feel if someone did praise you. Don't think too hard, or judge your responses, or wonder what you "should" feel; any and all feelings are valid if they are true for you.

Before you read any further, please stop to make a note of your feelings on the next page. You could draw a symbol or a face if you prefer, rather than writing the words. On page 40 you will find a list of feelings that other parents have told us are true for them. Do any match yours? When we do this activity in the groups, many parents are surprised by how many feelings we come up with, and are glad to find that other people often feel the same way as they do.

Most of us, when we were children, received many more negative and critical comments than we did positive and encouraging ones. With the best of intentions, many adults point out to children what they're doing wrong far more often than what they're doing right.

This negative attitude can have a big impact on us. When we think about our childhood, it can be painful to remember the harsh things we were told, and how we felt about them. It can also be painful to think about what we may be saying to our children, and how they may be feeling. We deserve kindness as much as they do, so take a break now if you need to.

When someone praises me, I feel...

......................................................................................................

......................................................................................................

......................................................................................................

When someone criticises me, I feel...

......................................................................................................

......................................................................................................

......................................................................................................

**(?) What occurs to you when you think about your feelings and look at the lists over the page?**

Almost everyone seems to feel angry or in some way upset when they are criticised, and only a few people say they find it useful and learn from it. It can lower our mood even to look at the list of painful feelings that criticism provokes. For some ideas on guiding without arousing these difficult feelings, see page 41.

When we are praised, many of us feel awkward or embarrassed, though many people also feel very positive. If we're not used to being appreciated for what we do or who we are, it can feel really uncomfortable at first – and can feel as though the other person is lying to us.

Do you think this is true of children and teenagers, too? When we ask this question in the groups, the answer is usually along the lines of "Yes – but even more so!" Everyone needs praise and encouragement, even if it's not always easy to accept. If your child rejects praise, don't be put off and give up. Think of a dried-up sponge: if you hold it under a fast flow of water, the water splashes off. If you slowly drip water onto it, the sponge softens, and can then absorb more water. With praise, little and often works best; keeping your praise specific and making it low-key will help the other person to accept it.

| When someone praises me, <br><br> **I feel...** | When someone criticises me, <br><br> **I feel...** |
|---|---|
| ready for anything | resentful |
| proud | depressed |
| glad | angry |
| a bit suspicious | inferior |
| energetic | lonely |
| happy | stupid |
| confident | ashamed |
| embarrassed | frustrated |
| relieved | small |
| like doing more | unloved |
| capable | sad |
| awkward | tearful |
| positive | no good |
| like I've grown | embarrassed |
| excited | want to prove them wrong |
| manipulated | stupid |
| shy | I want revenge |
| valued | inadequate |
| recognised | negative |
| worthwhile | rejected |
| uncomfortable | grateful if it's useful |
| loved | like giving up |
| uncertain | tired |
| great | defensive |
| stupid | misunderstood |
| delighted | miserable |

If it comes as a surprise to you that so many people have strong feelings about being criticised, and that most of us prefer praise and encouragement, you may want to look back to Session 1 and think some more about praising effectively.

# Guiding without criticising

Children and teenagers need our guidance while they are growing up. When we guide them without criticising, we separate the behaviour we see from the child as a person. We give them information about how to improve without being destructive. Criticism doesn't usually do any of these things.

### criticising

### Guiding

### criticising

### Guiding

## criticising

- hurts
- blames
- creates anger and defiance
- attacks the child rather than sorting out what they are doing
- fails to tell the child how to improve

## Guiding

- shows respect
- helps children to listen
- gives useful information
- encourages co-operation
- leads to shared ideas
- encourages change

We want to motivate and encourage children, to avoid discouragement and the damaging feelings that went with criticism in the list we've just been thinking about.

## What is it that motivates us?

Research shows that noticing and appreciating children's effort (this is sometimes referred to as process praise) is a more effective way of motivating them than praising them for being clever or "really good at maths." If we call them clever or good at something too often, it becomes an unhelpful form of labelling, as we discussed in the previous session.

We want children to believe that if they keep trying, they can do better. So we need to notice their efforts to understand, to do new things, or things which are hard for them. We want to encourage them to persist and to concentrate.

## Imagine a child struggling to put a jumper on:

| criticising | Guiding/ motivating |
|---|---|
| "Let's see what you're doing, Sam. | "How are you getting on Sam? |
| Dear me, you are getting into a muddle... | You're working really hard at getting that jumper on straight... You're nearly there! |
| You're usually good at getting dressed, but you've been doing that for ages and you're making a right mess of it. | What would happen if you put your arm through here? |
| Come here, let me do it. | Yes, that's a good idea... How does that feel? |
| We haven't got all day." | Well done. You worked really hard at that." |

# A Chart for Kindness

It's easy to get into the habit of noticing only what's going wrong in the family, the things that annoy us, the times children try our patience. The children do it too – telling us when their brother or sister or friend has done something they feel upset about but not when someone has been kind to them or they've been having fun. It can be hard for all of us to remember to spot the everyday kind and helpful things, rather than taking them for granted.

Here's a way of making this easier. Have a simple, colourful kindness chart. Whenever anyone spots someone else doing something kind or helpful, the person being kind is invited to add to the chart. Adults can nominate each other as well as children; children can nominate each other and grown-ups too. Visitors can be invited to join in. When you all get good at noticing for each other, you can start nominating yourselves as well.

Parents tell us that when they start looking out for all the good things that are happening in the family, they often notice that there are more of them than they thought! At first we may need to play a kindness "I Spy" game. Explain the idea to other family members – and then get it going yourself by noticing as much as you can. They'll soon follow your example (and if anyone doesn't, don't bother too much – just keep going).

The chart is not meant to be a competition. There shouldn't be individual lines of stars or smiley faces, as this is likely to result in one child getting smug and another with their nose out of joint for "losing". Everyone does their best and contributes to a general chart – just as they can contribute generally to having a positive atmosphere in the family.

**?** **What might we look out for? Here are some ideas.**
**What else can you think of that people do for each other in your family?**

| | |
|---|---|
| helping a sibling with their shoes | remembering to be quiet when someone is ill |
| feeding pets | taking out the rubbish |
| putting away the shopping | reading a story to/playing a game with a |
| tidying up without being asked | younger brother or sister |
| being patient | making you a cup of tea |
| cooking a nice meal | remembering to buy something for someone |
| helping to lay the table | being grateful or appreciative |

Here are some ideas for kindness charts. Keep them simple – and they don't have to be works of art! If you have children who enjoy drawing, they could take it in turns to design the chart for everyone to colour in. You can also buy stars and stickers quite cheaply in stationery shops.

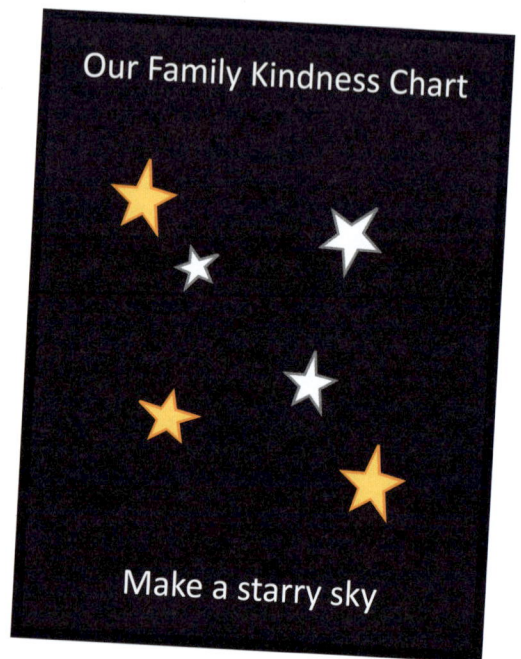

Our Family Kindness Chart

Bring a ray of sunshine

Our Family Kindness Chart

Spot the kindness

Our Family Kindness Chart

Wave the family flag

Our Family Kindness Chart

Make a starry sky

If you like you can have a go at designing your own Kindness Chart…

# The Question of Discipline

The word "discipline" is so often used to mean punishment that the idea of positive discipline may at first seem strange.
The word has the same origin as the word "disciple" – a follower, Someone who is guided. In The Nurturing Programme we think of it in this way: discipline is a system for guiding children, not for punishing them.

What is the point of disciplining children? We think they need our help to learn an important set of skills, ones that will be useful to them all their lives. These include the ability to give and take – to think about other people's needs as well as their own; skills in relating well to other people; taking responsibility for their own actions and honouring promises. And of course they need to learn how look after themselves in practical ways, rather than staying dependent on others. So discipline is a means to an end, rather than an end in itself, a way of helping children grow up as confident, independent, responsible and responsive people.

Unlike a car or a new washing machine, children aren't pre-programmed. Nor do they come into the world having read an instruction manual on behaviour – which is just as well, as no two families, no two schools, no two communities are exactly the same. This does mean that the adults need to be clear, so children know what is expected of them; to be patient, as it takes time to learn these skills; and to allow children to develop their own personality and preferences, too. None of this is easy!

We can force children to be obedient – we are bigger and more powerful than them. But in the long term it is more helpful for them to learn to co-operate through understanding and self-discipline, not because they are afraid of us.

what if punishment is the only thing that makes children behave?

"Usually we punish children when we can't think what else to do, or when we're so angry we lose control.

We'll be exploring lots of other ideas on how to help children learn to behave well."

# Boundaries: Setting Limits

In The Nurturing Programme we have identified four main kinds of boundaries that children and teenagers are likely to meet.

## constricting

Lots of rules and regulations, often backed up with severe punishments, little room to explore, do-as-you're-told – like a dictatorship

## inconsistent

Often a mixture of constricting and absent – strict one day and indulgent or neglectful the next

## Absent

No limits, anything goes, neglectful or indulgent – like anarchy

## clear, consistent

Safe, fair limits with clear expectations, stability with plenty of room to explore and grow – like a democracy

Most of us had to cope with different boundaries – maybe one parent was strict and the other indulgent, or a step-parent, grandparent, carer or childminder all had different ideas; boundaries at school, at clubs, church or mosque may have been different from those at home.

We have talked about boundaries with hundreds of people. Here is what they tell us – does it match your experience?

## constricting

If we are constricted and over-controlled, we may become rebellious and unco-operative, or go to the other extreme and become timid, submissive, waiting to be told what to do and reluctant to try things for fear of making mistakes.

## Absent

Too much freedom can be as scary as not having enough. If there are no boundaries, we may feel that nobody cares about us, and may behave in extreme and sometimes dangerous ways in an attempt to get someone to take charge.

## Inconsistent

With inconsistent boundaries we can feel confused and insecure, and also learn to be manipulative. If the adults around us aren't clear about what they expect of us, we can't learn what behaviour is OK – a lot of difficult behaviour can be traced to this.

## clear, consistent

Clear, fair boundaries help us feel secure, safe to explore within the limits and to test them; this leads to confidence, an ability to try things without taking foolish risks, and respect for others. These are helpful boundaries: consistency, particularly when we are young, is important.

**?** **Which of these boundaries do you identify with?**

**The ones that feel familiar are probably those you knew as a child. There's space on the next page for you to record your experiences.**

Boundaries I had as a child.................................................................................

..........................................................................................................................

How I felt... ........................................................................................................

..........................................................................................................................

..........................................................................................................................

How I behaved...................................................................................................

..........................................................................................................................

..........................................................................................................................

**?** **When you have thought about your own childhood, ask yourself what boundaries you think your child or children are experiencing – at home with you, and elsewhere in their lives – and record these ideas as well.**

**?** **Take time to reflect on how alike or how different your children's experiences are from your own, and why this may be so.**

Boundaries my children have (may be different for each child)...

..........................................................................................................................

..........................................................................................................................

How they may feel....................................................................................

..........................................................................................................................

..........................................................................................................................

How they may behave... .................................................................................

..........................................................................................................................

# Thinking about consistency

*Why is consistency important? Here are some examples of inconsistency.*

### yesterday

*What a wonderful game – that's a great way to play on a rainy afternoon!*

### Today

*How dare you make such a mess. I tidied the room specially as Gran is coming to tea.*

### Tomorrow

*Mum, we're bored.*

*Why don't you go and make a den with the cushions like you did the other day?*

### yesterday

*I'm so hungry – I need my tea.*

*You must put your bike away before you have tea.*

### Today

*I'm so hungry – I need my tea.*

*OK. I'll put your bike away for you after tea.*

### Tomorrow

*How dare you leave your bike out in the rain! Go and put it in the shed – now!*

**?** **How do you think the children might feel in these situations?**

**?** **What do they learn? What might they learn if the parent was clear about what was OK and what was not OK?**

**?** **You might like to think about ways in which you are consistent and inconsistent, and what the results are in your family.**

# What we Mean by Discipline

Let's be clear about the two kinds of discipline: positive and negative.

## ☺ Positive discipline

Positive discipline is encouraging. It makes allowances for the fact that children need time to learn what behaviour is OK and what is not, and that they will make mistakes. It pays attention to what they are doing well, rather than noticing only what they do wrong. It keeps adults in charge, while respecting children's rights and feelings and helping them to think and act for themselves. Its aim is to help children learn self-discipline, to take responsibility for their own actions, and to treat both others and themselves with care and respect.

**Here are some key ingredients in positive discipline:**

- it establishes and maintains clear boundaries

- it notices and rewards positive behaviour

- it uses reasonable penalties in response to negative behaviour

Positive discipline has a positive effect on children and teenagers: it shows them how to improve their behaviour without making them feel that they themselves are bad.

## ☹ Negative discipline

Negative discipline focuses on what children are doing wrong. It relies for control on children's fear of adults' power. Its methods are unfair, harsh and often inconsistent, and are based on punishment. It teaches what is wrong, but seldom explains what is right or acknowledges good behaviour.

Negative discipline has a negative effect on children: it makes them believe not just that they have done wrong, but that they themselves are bad.

There's another approach that, while it is not harsh, is also unhelpful. Over-indulgent and "marshmallow" attitudes (all soft and sweet!) tend to make children selfish and disrespectful.

### ☹ Negative discipline

### ☺ Positive discipline

### ☹ Negative discipline

### ☺ Positive discipline

# Types of Discipline

## Positive:

**Fair, firm, consistent, kind...**

clear and reasonable rules

open, flexible attitude

giving fair choices (with consequences)

negotiating

ignoring behaviour (not the child)

listening to all sides of the argument

### Rewards

praise

kind touch

extra story

treat

responsibility

encouragement

extra pocket money

extra games

extra time together

### Penalties

grounding

loss of privilege

parental disappointment

"paying back" for damage

less/no TV

removing toy/ game

loss of treats

## Negative:

**Unfair, critical, inconsistent, harsh...**

unclear or unreasonable rules

rigid or indulgent attitude

criticism

put-downs

ignoring child

using guilt

anger

giving in sometimes

bribery

humiliation

ridicule

favouring one child

### Punishments...

shouting

hitting

smacking

shaking

locking in/out

unreasonable grounding

threats

### Extra ideas you have...

### Extra ideas you have...

# Time to Calm Down

**Time to Calm Down is a way of helping children – and adults – when emotions are running high, a cooling-off period that gives everyone a chance to calm down.**

Parents are the emotional thermometer for the family and need to be able to model a calm response for children to learn from. Time to Calm Down helps us to hold onto clear boundaries without nagging, or adding our own angry outbursts to those of the children. We look in more detail at how to deal with anger in Session 5.

Time to Calm Down works best if parents have managed to learn to stay calm with babies, toddlers, young children and young people as they grow through the stages, although it is never too late to learn.

If older children have experienced a helpful approach to taking Time to Calm Down when they were young, they can take themselves away for their own Time to Calm Down. Children who learn to take Time to Calm Down for themselves when they need to deserve praise for learning to manage their feelings and behaviour. Time to Calm Down should not be humiliating or scary for the child – it is meant to be a calming-down strategy, not a harsh punishment.

Isn't Time to Calm Down the same as being put in the corner or shut away in another room? My parents did that when they were angry with me, and it felt terrible.

"Time to Calm Down is meant to be different. If you give Time to Calm Down when you are still calm, using it for specific ways of behaving, rather than giving it at random when you are cross, and if you keep it short, it does not feel humiliating or rejecting. Staying close to a young child during Time to Calm Down, but without touching or giving eye contact, also helps.

It is important to try and work out what triggers the child's anger or frustration, and to help with this in other ways too."

# Steps for Supporting Time to Calm Down

**1**   Stop what you are doing

**2**   Pause to calm yourself, step back, take a deep breath, have a quick glass of water

**3**   Give your full attention to your child, seek eye contact at their level and listen

**4**   Empathise with the feeling, even if the behaviour isn't acceptable, e.g. "I can see you are feeling really angry, and it's not okay to hit out at someone"

**5**   Say " it's time to calm down" in a calm voice, followed by "I'm here to help you." Repeat these as necessary, quietly and calmly

**6**   Some children may benefit from a safe, calming place, e.g. a big cushion or a little den to recover

**7**   Stay with them if they need your help to calm themselves

**8**   Think about a calming visual object to help recovery, or some calming music or sounds

**9**   If they are hurting themselves or others, place a gentle hand over theirs and say "no, I can't let you do that"

**10**   Welcome them whenever they are ready to re-join what is happening

# ☺ Making Time to Calm Down Work

# ☺ Making Time to Calm Down Work

Some children find it hard to calm down and may need to release frustration or anger safely before they can either calm down themselves or be helped by parents to become calm. Sending a child away as a punishment for angry or frustrated outbursts gives a message to children that their strong, difficult feelings are not welcome or they may feel rejected humiliated or scared. The important message is that Time to Calm Down is meant to help them learn to cope with their strong feelings in a safe way.

Sometimes children may appear to calmly or deliberately choose to hurt themselves or other people; they need to know that this is not okay, and they will need time away from an activity to recover.

## Top Tips in managing Time to Calm Down:

- Take time to explain Time to Calm Down so the child understands what will happen when strong feelings drive difficult behaviour

- Be fair, firm and consistent in keeping clear boundaries

- Find ways of being able to stay calm yourself

- Show you are interested in helping your child to manage their strong feelings so they can learn how to calm themselves down

- Think about what situations are likely to cause strong feelings and be prepared

- Notice what naturally calms your child and use it to help when strong feelings are building

- Be encouraging when a child has managed to stay calm and reinforce the activity that helped.

- Spend some Time In together to play or to listen to children and young people about their feelings or concerns.

There is often more than one child involved when strong feelings take over. Sometimes it is not easy to know exactly what has been going on, and in that case everyone needs to calm down before the problem can be solved respectfully.

It is very easy for the balance of giving more attention to positive than to negative behaviour to slip and result in more negative behaviour. For example, you could notice when feelings are building and distract them with play or ask them to help you with a task.

**Calming down activities to try:** Sipping a large glass of cold water / Singing / Have a hug / Visualising places associated with happy memories / Colouring in a book / Having a walk or run or other exercise / Play doh or plasticine play / Playing calming music / Closing eyes and deep breathing / Blowing up balloons / Blowing bubbles

Use this page to record your plans for introducing Time to Calm Down in the family.

# Practice Sheet
## Planning Time to Calm Down

Situations where you might want to use Time to Calm Down with your children:

.............................................................................................................

.............................................................................................................

What can I do to calm myself:

.............................................................................................................

.............................................................................................................

Calming places I can think of to encourage calming:

.............................................................................................................

What I can use as a calming visual object:

.............................................................................................................

What we might do together when Time to Calm Down is over:

.............................................................................................................

.............................................................................................................

What changes are you hoping to see in your child's behaviour?

.............................................................................................................

.............................................................................................................

.............................................................................................................

.............................................................................................................

# REFLECTIONS

All this talk about discipline has really set me thinking. But where do I start?

When I'm stressed I get impatient and critical. I'd never thought how the children might feel. I'm really going to try to be calmer and positive!

I'm confused about discipline being positive. It's so different from what I learned when I was a child - discipline just meant punishment.

I used to send my child to his room for Time to Calm Down. I'm going to try this new way of staying calm and see if it works.

We've packed a lot into this session. If what we're suggesting is very different from what happened to you when you were growing up it can feel strange, and a challenge to think about changing old ways. If you're already doing a lot of positive things, it's good to appreciate yourself, and to think about how to be even more helpful as a parent.

It's all very well for the others. I'm not sure I can change, or even that I want to.

Take your time to think about it, and about what changes you'd like to see in your family. There's no need to try everything at once! Maybe you'll start with encouraging the whole family to be kinder to each other. Or you could think about boundaries, and notice when you're giving mixed messages. If you find yourself nagging and then flying off the handle, you could decide to explain about Time to Calm Down, and try that. In the end, all The Nurturing Programme ideas work together, so start with whatever appeals to you.

# REFLECTIONS

**?** **What are you thinking and feeling at the end of the second session? If you would like to, record your own ideas here.**

............................................................................................

............................................................................................

............................................................................................

............................................................................................

# Time to Have a Go

SUN  MON  TUES  WED  THURS  FRI  SAT  SUN  MON  TUES  WED  THURS  FRI  SAT

Praise everyone in the family - including yourself.

Explain the idea of a kindness chart to the family, and start using one.

Talk to the children about Time to Calm Down, and think about what situations in the family it might be useful for.

Try to have extra Time In with your children - play a game, bake a cake, read an extra story, go for a walk, etc.

# Session 3: Parenting Styles and Family Rules

empathy helps
people to feel
understood

time to calm
down works
best when
parents are
calm too

praise
is magic

we're
on the
lookout for
kindness

# Feedback: What Parents Tell Us

### Praise

"I still feel awkward if someone says something kind to me, but I'm learning to say 'Thanks' and that makes it easier."

### Kindness chart

"It seems to work better if we remember to do it quite a lot so the chart is full up before the children get bored with it. The twins want to design the next chart themselves."

### Time to Calm Down

"I didn't realise you were meant to stay close by while the child took Time to Calm Down. It's working much better now I stay near her, and we're both shouting less so it's not needed so often."

### Time In

"If I can make time to play with the children, have fun with them, it seems to help them behave better the rest of the time. It's the days I'm busy and stressed that they behave the worst."

**?** **What have you tried so far, and how is it going? Make a note of how you're getting on if you'd like to.**

I had a go at...

and the result was...

# Parenting Styles

We have thought about the importance of empathy and praise for children, as well as the need for clear boundaries. In the following sessions we will be exploring more ways to keep the balance between warmth, encouragement and interest in our children, and clear structure, boundaries and expectations. This is often referred to as an **authoritative** parenting style and has been shown to be the best approach for helping children to grow up to be confident, competent and kind.

We know that it's not possible to get the balance right all the time; there is no such thing as a perfect parent. It may even be appropriate to have times when we're more indulgent, more detached or more authoritarian, what matters is the overall balance.

**All the evidence shows that the most effective parenting provides:**

- Both warmth and structure
- Age-appropriate independence
- Clear boundaries
- Interest, responsiveness and support

☺ **Authoritative**

I'd like you to be in by 9.00. It's an important school day tomorrow

But my friends are all coming back on the bus which gets in at 9.20

Ok. It's sensible to come back together. But please text me when you're on the bus.

Adults are adults and children are children, so shouldn't they just accept that what they have to do is different from what we do?

"It's true, in some ways we are different, and children accept that. They do, though, learn a lot of their behaviour and attitudes from us, and from other adults, so it's worth thinking about what behaviour we want from them, and then to model it in the way we behave to them."

**Less helpful styles are known as:**

## 🙁 Authoritarian

These parents have strict boundaries, but are not very responsive to children's needs and may find it harder to show warmth and affection.

"Do as I say because I say so."

## 🙁 Indifferent

These parents are not very responsive to children's needs for warmth and interest and also find it hard to provide clear structure and boundaries. They may have given up.

## 🙁 Indulgent or Permissive

These parents are warm and responsive but have few boundaries or expectations. They may try to be their young person's friend and want to avoid any disagreements or conflict.

We may all adopt different styles at different times but if your relationship with your child is not as you wish, think about whether there needs to be a shift in the balance. Do they need more nurturing and warmth or would clearer boundaries and expectations be helpful?

# Family Rules

In this session we look in detail at how to set up a family-friendly system that helps everyone feel safe and comfortable, and supports efforts to co-operate with the rules that are agreed.

Some people are uncomfortable with the idea of rules. You can replace the word rules with guidelines, agreement, contract or code – whatever suits you. The point is that children and teenagers need to know what we expect, to know where the boundaries are and to respect them, at least most of the time. To help them, keeping to the rules is rewarded, and breaking the rules is penalised.

A healthy family is like a mini-democracy. Parents are definitely in charge. At the same time, children have a voice: the right to express their views. Children whose opinions are respected find it easier to accept decisions even when they don't get their own way. It's people who feel powerless who start revolutions!

One way children learn how to behave is by copying others around them. We often say to children, "Do as I say!" They are more likely to do as we do! We may not like it when we notice that they are shouting, or swearing, or leaving their plates on the table; without realising it, we often teach them to do these things because we do them ourselves. In the same way as the captain of a football team has to abide by the rules of the game as well as all the other team members (and may be shown the red card if he breaks a rule) so it is best to have some rules that apply to grown-ups as well as children.

Isn't it a good thing for the kids to learn that the world's an unfair place?

"You're right they will have to cope with this when they're older. It does help, though, if they experience clear, consistent, fair rules when they are growing up, particularly if they are allowed to contribute to what happens in the family. Then they will be able to think for themselves when the world offers confusing alternatives."

*Here's a chance to think about how things are going in the family.*

**?** **How do you feel and how do you think others in the family may be feeling?**

**?** **What's happening that causes friction, anger, nagging – things you might like to handle differently or change for the better?**

**?** **What rules are there already in the family (they may not be clear or spelt out), and how well do they work?**

How do we want to feel at home?

............................................................................................

............................................................................................

............................................................................................

Family issues that get in the way of good feelings

............................................................................................

............................................................................................

............................................................................................

............................................................................................

Rules (said and unsaid) we already have in our house - and how well they work

............................................................................................

............................................................................................

............................................................................................

**?** **When you have finished, compare your ideas with the examples other parents have given us. Do you have some ideas in common?**

### How do we want to feel at home?

happy

able to make mistakes

loved

listened to

accepted for who I am

relaxed

respected

valued

liked

understood

safe

able to be honest about different feelings

### Family issues that get in the way of good feelings:

shouting and screaming

having to nag before children take any notice

rows, moody silences

fighting

use of TV

swearing

sharing toys, etc.

criticism, put-downs

mealtimes

bedtime

getting up in the morning

helping with chores

running/stamping around the house

tidying up

privacy (for older children and teenagers)

taking things without asking

noise level of music

violence

# Dos and Don'ts

Having thought about how we'd like to feel, and what sort of things make it difficult for us to enjoy these good feelings, let's work out some rules that can help everyone in the family behave in ways that allow us to feel at ease.

In The Nurturing Programme we give each rule in two ways: as a DO and as a DON'T. When we want someone to do something, it often seems easier to tell them not to do something that we don't like, rather than thinking of what we do like and asking them to do it. For the other person, it's much harder when we tell them this way. See what happens when we say "Don't".

**Don't** *think of a kangaroo!*

We can't help thinking of a kangaroo. Our brains can't work out negative instructions – when they hear the word "kangaroo", up the picture comes. Only then can the brain try to obey the instruction, and by then it's too late! This is true in other situations, too.

### Don't

*Here's your bun.* **Don't** *drop it!*

### Do

*Here's your bun.* **Hold it** *tight!*

If we say, *"Don't drop it",* the child's brain has to work out the meaning of what we say (and is likely to react to the word "drop") before deciding what needs to be done instead. A simple "Hold tight" lets the brain send the right message to the muscles straight away.

This is true when we give advice, and it's also true when we're reminding children about rules.

😞 **Don't**

😊 **DO**

😞 **Don't**     😊 **DO**

If we are clear about what we want, the child or teenager is more likely to do as we ask. If we just tell them to stop what they're doing, they may ignore us, be confused – or choose to outsmart us.

*If we emphasise the* **DO***, and have the* **DON'T** *as a backup, the rule will be clear – and it's easier to remember.*

*Here are some examples of **DO** and **DON'T** rules, designed to sort out some of the issues listed on page 70.*

## DO

**Do** listen when someone is talking to you

**Do** put your coat, shoes, etc. away when you come in

**Do** stay at the table once meals have started

**Do** be gentle with each other

**Do** ask before borrowing something

**Do** play ball games outside

## Don't

**Don't** ignore or interrupt a person talking to you

**Don't** leave your things lying around

**Don't** leave the table in the middle of meals

**Don't** hurt, hit or bite each other

**Don't** take anyone else's things without asking

**Don't** play ball games in the house

**Do you get the idea?!** When we make rules with the family, it's a good idea to display the list somewhere as a reminder. Make the rules chart attractive and colourful. If you have young children, draw pictures of the rules as well as a list.

## Dos

Do listen when someone is talking to you

Do put your coat, shoes, etc. away when you come in

Do stay at the table once meals have started

## Don'ts

Don't ignore or interrupt a person talking to you

Don't leave your things lying around

Don't leave the table in the middle of meals

# Thinking About our Family Rules

Before we introduce a new idea to other people, it can be helpful to practise it ourselves. It's hard to be clear with others unless we're sure we've understood what to do. So, before you try talking about rules with the family, we suggest you have a go on your own. If you have a partner or share your flat or house with other adults, it would be a good idea to have a chat with them about the idea of introducing rules for the family.

Of course, when you talk about rules as a family, you may decide together on quite different ones. That's fine – it needs to be a joint effort.

It is fair, and much easier for children (particularly as they get older) to accept rules if they are given some say, and if some of the rules apply to everyone in the family, not just to children. For example, a rule about shouting or swearing, borrowing or tidiness, should apply to everyone; a bedtime rule would apply to children only.

## we suggest you:

☐ turn back to page 69, where you listed how you and your family would like to feel, and ways family members behave that get in the way of these good feelings

☐ think of what behaviour you'd like instead of the unwanted behaviour. Be very specific, and also be realistic about the rules according to the age of your child or children (a three-year-old can't do the washing up!)

☐ turn a few of these ideas into DO and DON'T rules, making sure you include some that apply to adults as well as children

On the page opposite, there's a practice sheet for you to note your ideas. At this stage, just list your suggestions for rules you'd like to have – we'll come back to the rewards and penalties later.

The steps for agreeing rules with the family, and another sheet to record the rules you would all like to have, are given later in the session.

# Practice Sheet
## Thinking About our Family Rules

### DOs

**1** .............................................................
.............................................................
.............................................................

Reward .............................................................
.............................................................
.............................................................

**2** .............................................................
.............................................................
.............................................................

Reward .............................................................
.............................................................
.............................................................

**3** .............................................................
.............................................................
.............................................................

Reward .............................................................
.............................................................
.............................................................

**4** .............................................................
.............................................................
.............................................................

Reward .............................................................
.............................................................
.............................................................

### Don'ts

**1** .............................................................
.............................................................
.............................................................

Penalty .............................................................
.............................................................
.............................................................

**2** .............................................................
.............................................................
.............................................................

Penalty .............................................................
.............................................................
.............................................................

**3** .............................................................
.............................................................
.............................................................

Penalty .............................................................
.............................................................
.............................................................

**4** .............................................................
.............................................................
.............................................................

Penalty .............................................................
.............................................................
.............................................................

# Rewards and Penalties

**It's all very well having rules. How can we reinforce them in a fair, positive way, so we build children's confidence and help them feel capable, rather than knocking it down so they feel inadequate?**
*(Think back to the feelings connected with praise and criticism that we explored in Session 2.)*

Children often want to please us, but not always, and some of the ways we want them to behave don't come naturally to them. Can you remember trying to change a habit of your own? Did you find it easy?

If the children – or we – have got into bad habits, it helps to break the habit and begin to learn a new one if something pleasant happens when we remember to change what we do. Having simple rewards that recognise our efforts also helps us to look out for success – in the same way as a kindness chart helps everyone in the family to notice when someone is being kind. This is balanced by having a penalty when a rule is broken.

Some people think that children shouldn't be rewarded for their efforts. But which of us would do our jobs without being paid? And would the World Cup or the Olympic Games be the same without trophies and medals? We learn more quickly and easily if we have goals, and if our efforts are appreciated.

We can probably all recognise this from our own experience. Science has caught up with us, and can now tell us that different chemicals are released in the brain when we have an enjoyable experience or an unpleasant experience. These help to code events in our memory. The coding for enjoyable events motivates us to repeat the experience. So if we want children to do something, they're more likely to remember to do it if something nice happens – if we notice and reward their efforts.

**Won't children get spoilt, and expect a reward for everything, for ever?**

**'It doesn't seem to work that way. Children enjoy feeling capable. Once they've learned a good habit, they don't need to be rewarded any longer though they still like to be thanked for what they do; and that's also true of us as adults."**

# Choosing Rewards and Penalties

Rewards and penalties should be linked to the rule they are helping to enforce. Children easily understand the logic of this, and it helps to reinforce the rule more effectively.

## Reward

*Thank you for remembering our sharing rule. You can each add a sticker to the reward chart.*

## Penalty

*You forgot the sharing rule. The penalty is playing in separate rooms.*

It's also a good idea to choose rewards that really mean something in your family. In one family, everyone loved the idea of eating by candlelight (and all the children were old enough to light candles safely), so that was agreed as the reward for the "help at mealtimes" rule.

## Reward

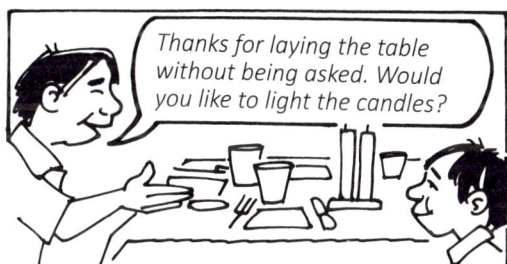

*Thanks for laying the table without being asked. Would you like to light the candles?*

## Penalty

*Nobody remembered to come and help lay the table for tea, so no candles today.*

If the whole family wants to work together to earn something special (like a trip to the zoo, going swimming or having a pond in the garden), you could have just one reward for keeping to all the rules.

Modest rewards are a good incentive, and not earning a reward is often enough of a penalty. And rewards don't always need to involve spending money: a walk in the park or extra time playing a game together, for instance. You can offer as a reward an outing that you had planned to take the children on anyway. You don't need to promise the earth to get children to co-operate!

# Rules, Rewards and Penalties

Here is a reward and a penalty you could have for each of the rules we suggested on page 73. Some have been chosen to apply to both adults and children.

## 🙂 DOS

**DO** listen when someone is talking to you

**Reward:** Colour a square on the Listening Ear - new music for car journeys

**DO** be gentle with each other

**Reward:** Star on the kindness chart

**DO** put your coat, shoes, etc. away when you come in

**Reward:** Remember for a week, and we'll fly the kite at the weekend

**DO** stay at the table during meals

**Reward:** Putting dried pasta in a jar, and a special meal when the jar is full

**DO** ask before borrowing something

**Reward:** A happier family atmosphere - and you'll probably be able to borrow it again

**DO** play ball games in the garden

**Reward:** Earn points towards buying a sports poster (or even tickets for a match)

## 🙁 Don'ts

**Don't** ignore or interrupt a person talking to you

**Penalty:** No square on the Listening Ear

**Don't** hurt, hit or bite each other

**Penalty:** Children: Time to Calm Down
Adults: Time to Calm Down

**Don't** leave your things lying around

**Penalty:** No kite-flying at the weekend

**Don't** leave the table during meals

**Penalty:** No additions to the jar

**Don't** take anyone else's things without asking

**Penalty:** You can't borrow it next time

**Don't** play ball games in the house

**Penalty:** Ball is confiscated for the day

# Rewards and Penalties for our Family

We listed some possible rewards and penalties in Session 2 when we were thinking about types of discipline. Look back to page 53 to remind you of these, and of the extra ideas you added to the list. Then turn to page 75, and add a reward and penalty to each of the rules you might like for your family. Make the rewards and penalties relevant to each rule. They will need to be more specific than our examples. For instance, what treat completing a star chart would earn; how much extra pocket money would be given, and so on.

When you come to discuss rules, rewards and penalties with your family, the rules may change to meet the whole family's needs, and they will have ideas about suitable rewards and penalties, too. When these have all been agreed, and the rules chart has been colourfully designed, everyone could sign it, or add a handprint, thumb print or other symbol, so all of you "own" the rules.

## To make this system successful, remember to:

☐ involve the whole family in the process (could the children design reward charts?) join in the system yourself: you are the family role model!

☐ be as consistent as you can

☐ pay more attention to Dos and rewards than Don'ts and penalties

☐ reward little and often, and with young children as soon as they have made a choice to keep to a rule

☐ divide the day (e.g. getting up and having breakfast/going to school/ coming home and teatime/teatime to bedtime) so young children can earn rewards without having to remember the rule all day long

☐ make rewards achievable - e.g. complete a chart in a week or so, don't let It drag on till everyone is bored with it

The goal is for children to learn to behave co-operatively and to learn self-discipline because it feels good. Then the feelings themselves come to provide an "intrinsic" reward, as family life becomes more relaxed and enjoyable.

# Steps for Making Family Rules

**1** **Get everyone to join in**
*Suggest that as you all live under one roof, you need to agree rules for everyone. If a child won't join in you can point out that they will miss the chance to have their say, and that rules will be agreed that will apply to them too.*

**2** **Talk about how you want to feel in the family**
*Encourage everyone to share their ideas*

**3** **Share problem behaviour**
*Ask everyone to talk freely – without fault-finding and blaming – about issues the family could improve.*

**4** **Share ideas for rules**
*Identify issues you would all like to have as rules in your family. For every behaviour you do not want, think of a behaviour you would like instead. Fill in the practice sheet "Our Family Rules" as you go along, and then produce your own colourful version.*

**5** **Keep the rules simple and specific**
*Rules need to be clear, easy to understand, and realistic. Avoid rules such as "Do be good – Don't be naughty" or "Do be happy – Don't be sad/angry".*

**6** **Decide on a reward and a penalty for each rule**
*For family rules such as "Do talk nicely to each other – Don't shout", children will accept the rule more readily if parents respect it too, and agree to a suitable reward and penalty for themselves. Let children as well as adults suggest rewards and penalties.*

**7** **Limit family rules**
*A maximum of four or five rules is plenty. Keeping the list short will help everyone remember the rules and practise them.*

**8** **Drop and add new rules when needed**
*Rules are not cast in concrete. When something is no longer a problem, have a rule-dropping party!*

# Practice Sheet
## Our Family Rules

### DOs

1 ................................................
................................................
................................................

Reward ....................................
................................................
................................................

2 ................................................
................................................
................................................

Reward ....................................
................................................
................................................

3 ................................................
................................................
................................................

Reward ....................................
................................................
................................................

4 ................................................
................................................
................................................

Reward ....................................
................................................
................................................

### Don'ts

1 ................................................
................................................
................................................

Penalty ...................................
................................................
................................................

2 ................................................
................................................
................................................

Penalty ...................................
................................................
................................................

3 ................................................
................................................
................................................

Penalty ...................................
................................................
................................................

4 ................................................
................................................
................................................

Penalty ...................................
................................................
................................................

# REFLECTIONS

I've always wanted to be kinder in bringing up my son, but thought if I was soft on him he'd run riot. But it sounds as though I can be firm without giving him a hard time.

It's not fair. Why should my children have an easy time when I had to do what my parents said without anyone thinking about my feelings?

I still don't think children should be rewarded all the time. But I suppose if I limit it to little things, it'll be all right I'll give it a go and see what happens.

We don't ever really talk about things in our family. I wonder how they'll react when I say I want to talk about rules.

Some of the ideas in this session may challenge the way our families have behaved for generations. It can be quite hard to take the plunge and look at how we might do things differently. If partners are reluctant to take part, suggest that you want to try setting up rules, rewards and penalties as an experiment, and quietly go ahead. If they see it working, maybe they'll join in later.

Talking about family life can remind us about what happened to us when we were children. If these memories are uncomfortable, it's worth noticing how we feel – perhaps sad or angry, rebellious or helpless. These feelings, though painful, can help to motivate us, and help us make our children's experience different from our own. If what we remember fits in with these ideas, they can spur us on to keep up the good work, and support us during the inevitable blips when things aren't going so smoothly.

# REFLECTIONS

**?** **What are you thinking and feeling at the end of the third session? If you would like to, record your own ideas here.**

..................................................................................

..................................................................................

..................................................................................

..................................................................................

..................................................................................

# Time to Have a Go

SUN   MON   TUES   WED   THURS   FRI   SAT   SUN   MON   TUES   WED   THURS   FRI   SAT

Meet as a family to agree family rules, and to decide on rewards and penalties. Make the occasion fun, and celebrate your efforts (ice cream all round when you've finished?).

Keep praising family members and yourself.

Keep practising Time to Calm Down and check that you are enjoying some Time In together.

# Session 4: Personal Power and self-esteem, choices and consequences

what we pay attention to is what we get more of

empathy helps people to feel understood

time to calm down works best when parents are calm too

clear fair rules help us all feel safe

praise is magic

we're on the lookout for kindness

DOS work better than DON'TS

# Feedback: What Parents Tell Us

### Family Rules

"Talking about how we feel and what upsets us was a real eye-opener."

### Time to Calm Down

"I understand now why it's important to use Time to Calm Down consistently and not just to get the kids out of the way when I can't cope with them any more. When that happens, it's me that needs the Time to Calm Down, not them!"

### Praise

"I still can't praise myself out loud, but it's getting easier to do it in my head."

### Family Rules

"I think I've realised that I used to notice what the kids did wrong much more than I did when they behaved well. Having the DOs and rewards helps me as well as them- and I've noticed a difference already."

### Family Rules

"My older son thought the idea was stupid, but the rest of us went ahead anyway."

**?** **What have you tried so far, and how is it going?**
**Make a note of how you're getting on if you'd like to.**

I had a go at...

and the result was...

# Introducing Personal Power, Self-esteem and Choices and Consequences

The three topics in this session are closely linked. **Personal power** is about feeling strong inside – it's our emotional strength rather than our physical strength. **Self-esteem** is the way we feel about ourselves – we can feel confident, positive, likeable (high self-esteem), or inadequate, stupid, bad (low self-esteem). If our self-esteem is healthy, we're likely to use our personal power well and make good **choices** in our lives; if our self-esteem is low, it's much harder to do this. If we make poor choices, it's likely that we'll end up feeling worse about ourselves.

So all three parts combine to influence the way we behave. You could think of them as a triangle, like this.

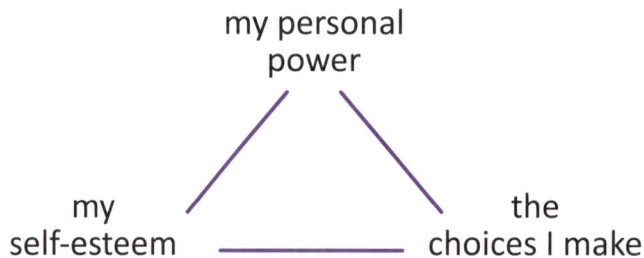

**Imagine you're out shopping, and you see someone you know. You think they've seen you, too, but they ignore you. Here are two reactions we might have.**

Notice how the way we're feeling (our self-esteem) affects what we do about the situation (using our personal power to choose how to behave).

*Oh dear, I must have upset her for her to cut me dead. Perhaps she doesn't really like me but it's rude just to walk off anyway, so I'm not going to bother to say hello to her next time.*

*That's strange, she's usually so friendly. Maybe she didn't see me – or maybe she's worried about something. I'll call her when I get home to make sure she's all right.*

# Personal Power

**Personal power is the emotional strength we have to get our needs met, and to make choices in our lives. It isn't about being physically strong, or about having power over other people. It's our inner strength – power for ourselves, not power against others. This idea is new to many people, so we will spend some time exploring it.**

The power itself is neutral. We can choose to use it in a positive way or a negative way. It is much easier to use our personal power well by making positive choices if we have positive, healthy self-esteem. Even if we are feeling low, when we remember our Personal Power and can manage to use it well to make choices that have good results, we will find we give our self-esteem a boost.

If we're going to feel safe and in charge of our lives, we all need to feel that we have some power. Babies have very little power; they need other people to do everything for them, and don't understand enough to make choices deliberately. As children grow older, they gradually need to have more power, more choice. They need adults to help them learn to use their power well. Sometimes we can feel as though we don't have power. Then we may feel angry, rebellious and resentful, or perhaps helpless, inadequate and depressed. However we react, feeling powerless tends to fuel low self-esteem and negative behaviour.

Encouraging children to use their personal power is a way of helping them learn to be respectful and thoughtful, towards others and also towards themselves. It isn't the same as letting them do whatever they want – being rude or irresponsible or refusing to help with chores. Some children have too much power over others, and are allowed to rule the roost. This isn't good for them either!

**Surely sometimes you are powerless, like when you're stuck in a traffic jam, or if you are made redundant?**

**"Yes, it's true that we sometimes don't have power over a situation. We do still have the power to choose how we react to it – what we do to cope with the situation we're in."**

Here are some unhelpful and some helpful ways of using personal power.

☹ **Unhelpful**          ☺ **Helpful**

☹ **Unhelpful**          ☺ **Helpful**

☹ **Unhelpful**          ☺ **Helpful**

Let's think some more about areas in our lives where we have power, and how we might choose to use it. There are seldom right or wrong answers, and what's helpful for one person (dressing fashionably, perhaps) could be unhelpful for another (if they don't enjoy it, and dress up only to please others). What matters is being aware that we are choosing what we do. Remember, too, that personal power doesn't depend on external power (e.g. having lots of money), it's how we deal with the situation we're in (if money's short, buying a few essentials each week to spread the cost would be a good use of our power.)

**These are just a few examples. Please add some of your own areas of power, and what for you would be unhelpful and helpful uses of your power.**

## Areas in our lives in which we have power

| Helpful use (+) | | Unhelpful use (-) |
|---|---|---|
| **mostly healthy, with treats** | what we eat | **all-junk food, or rigid diet** |
| **in time to get enough sleep** | when we go to bed | **always watching late-night TV** |
| **staying in budget** | spending money | **reckless spending** |
| **making time to be with people we have fun with, and who are supportive** | our friends | **being with people who are unkind or use us; neglecting friends** |
| **regular times to do what we enjoy** | leisure time | **not making time for any!** |
| **exercise routine for fun and health** | fitness | **never taking any exercise; or being obsessive about it** |
| **making up our own minds** | how we vote | **doing what family/partner always does** |
| ................................. | ................................. | ................................. |
| ................................. | ................................. | ................................. |
| ................................. | ................................. | ................................. |

# Power and powerlessness

We all have a sense of being powerless sometimes. At other times we are comfortably in charge. We have different feelings in these two situations. The Power Quiz on the next page gives examples of what we may feel when we have different amounts of power. Before reading on, please do the quiz.

> **?**  **Might children feel the same way as us when they're comfortable with power or are feeling powerless?**

*"The same, maybe even more so"* is an answer we often get to this question. For a child, as for us, it's also true that having too much power can feel scary or overwhelming (and occasionally exhilarating!).

> **?**  **How might children behave when they have some of these difficult feelings?**

We need to help children and teenagers recognise that they, like us, always have some power, their personal power, the power to choose how to behave even when they have no power over events. If they learn this, they will be less likely to suffer the negative effects of feeling powerless. We can talk to them about the idea of personal power, show them by using our own personal power well, and help them weigh up the choices they do have.

It is also helpful to children if they are given more power in their lives as they are growing up. The amount of independence and responsibility that's right for a 14-year-old is different from what a 4-year-old needs. If you take another look at the chart on page 91, you could ask yourself whether your children seem comfortable with the amount of power they have. Even little things – what colour socks they wear, or what (within reason) will go in the lunchbox – can make a big difference to them.

> **?**  **Might they benefit from having a bit more say in what happens to them? Or do they have too much power, too much choice, and more responsibility than they are ready to handle?**

You're the best judge of this for your own child. Look again at the lists of feelings in the Power Quiz. If children seem to be comfortable, they probably are. If there are a lot of power struggles in the family, perhaps everyone is feeling powerless, even if they seem to be demanding quite a lot of power! A greater sense of internal, personal power can, for any of us, reduce the need for external power, power over others.

**On the Power Quiz are some words to describe how we may feel in relation to power. Circle the feelings that are familiar to you. Can you think of others that haven't been included? You could add your extra ideas if you'd like to.**

# Power Quiz

**When I feel comfortable with the power I have, I also feel...**

in control     strong     competent     confident

patient     safe     positive     valued     capable

secure     helpful to others     decisive     clear

responsible     energetic     healthy     relaxed

**Extra ideas:** ....................................................................

....................................................................

....................................................................

....................................................................

**When I feel powerless, I also feel...**

defeated     overwhelmed     paralysed     violent

scared     frightened     tearful     anxious

defensive     like giving up     angry     depressed     insecure

helpless     rebellious     irresponsible     desperate

**Extra ideas:** ....................................................................

....................................................................

....................................................................

....................................................................

# Developing Personal Power

If we have a good sense of our own personal power, it's easier to help children develop theirs. It isn't surprising that we find it hard to share power with children. We may fear that they will walk all over us, that we need to be in control all the time. We can use control – our power over children – to get them to behave, but the price may be high. Our children's self-esteem and their sense of being capable and responsible will shrink rather than grow. Over-control encourages dependency and also rebellion, rather than self-discipline. We may find that we have to impose more and more control, resulting in more and more rebelliousness – a vicious circle that's hard to get out of for us and for the child.

It's quite right that as adults we should be in charge; that's not quite the same thing as having total control. It's a good use of our own personal power to help children and teenagers learn how to use theirs well.

**to develop a sense of personal power in ourselves we need to:**

- treat ourselves with respect

- take responsibility for the choices we make, and the results (consequences) that follow

- communicate honestly without blaming or criticising others

- look for the good in ourselves

- praise ourselves for being and doing

- be aware of our own needs and feelings

- honour commitments

- make healthy choices and helpful decisions

**to develop a sense of personal power in children we need to:**

- treat them with respect

- give them chances to succeed

- encourage them to take responsibility for the choices they make, and the results (consequences) that follow

- help them to become independent and competent

- praise them for being and doing

- listen and talk to them

- honour their feelings

- respect their body

- allow them to learn from their mistakes

- be nurturing and consistent in helping them learn how to behave well

# Self-esteem

**Self-esteem is the second bit of the triangle. The way we think and feel about ourselves – our self-esteem – is first shaped in childhood by the events we experience and the way we are treated.**

Self-esteem mirrors the way others seemed to think and feel about us. As adults, it can still be hard to feel positive about ourselves if others are often negative and critical of us. It's much harder for children. This was true for us when we were children, and it's true for our children. Here's a way of thinking about it:

how I think and
feel about myself

how others behave
towards me

how I behave
towards others

As children, we believe what adults say. They tell us, "The sun helps the vegetables to grow", and "That big grey animal? It's an elephant", and "Look out! Fire burns". If they say, "You'll never turn out any good" or "You're such fun", we believe that too. It's easy to think that if only our children would behave better, the problems we have with them would go away. But it may be that change needs to begin with how we and others behave towards them. And that can be tough, because if we're not feeling good about ourselves, it is hard for us to change, too.

So maybe we need to think about what we can do to boost our own self-esteem, as well as recognising the need to build self-esteem in our children. It's a really good use of our personal power to be kind to ourselves!

**Do you mean that we can't expect the kids to change unless we do?**

**"It certainly makes it much easier for them to change if we change too. As adults we need to take the lead. The important thing is to find ways to feel good about ourselves, and to help them feel that way too."**

# The Self-Esteem Climate

On the page opposite is a self-esteem "weather chart". On the left-hand side is stormy, cloudy weather; on the right-hand side is warm, sunny weather.

**Choose from the first list below words that you think reflect a stormy, difficult climate, and write them in box 1 on the left-hand side of the weather chart. Write words that reflect a warm, nurturing climate in box 2 on the right-hand side.**

mimicking / praise / teasing / fair rules / verbal abuse / negotiating / tying up trust / playing together / locking in / listening / coldness / empathy / rejection distrust / acceptance / inconsistency / no/too much responsibility / having fun ignoring child / not listening / understanding / no humour / hugs / no choice shared humour / no cuddles / threats / love / lack of approval / no praise consistency / nagging / favouritism / encouragement / put-downs / responsibility smacking / respect / no playing / kindness / criticism / clear boundaries labelling arrogance / explaining / shouting / fairness / neglect / sharing interests ignoring minor annoying behaviour / choices / no fun / rewards and penalties

**When you have done this, look at the words in the second list. These are examples of children's attitudes and behaviour. Again, write the words you think belong on the stormy side in box 3 on the left, and ones that belong on the sunny side in box 4 on the right. Compare your choices with the ones on the completed chart.**

fights / co-operates / headaches / confident / isolated / tries new things / tired angry / enthusiastic / bully / copes realistically with setbacks / bullied / listens stammering / energetic / whinging / makes friends easily / refusing to talk usually happy / won't try / usually healthy / depressed / glad to please / cries a lot often breaks rules / takes responsibility for own actions / guilty / relaxed / kind gives up easily / "I can't" / nail biting / empathic / rebellious / aggressive / resilient can't concentrate / tummyaches / very shy / assertive / disruptive / feels helpless stressed / respectful / introverted / can self-praise / too cheeky / praises others shouts / affectionate / hits/hurts others / smiles often / over-keen to please resolves problems peaceably / clingy / blames others / lonely / gang leader

**On page 99 you will find more ideas about this activity.**

# How To Increase Self-Esteem

## Boundaries * Listening * Praise * Fairness * Consistency

**1**

input
from others
affects
how we feel
about ourselves
and how
we behave

**2**

**3**

resulting
behaviour
and attitudes
in children

**4**

## All behaviour has a reason - it's trying to meet a need

# How To Increase Self-Esteem
## Boundaries * Listening * Praise * Fairness * Consistency

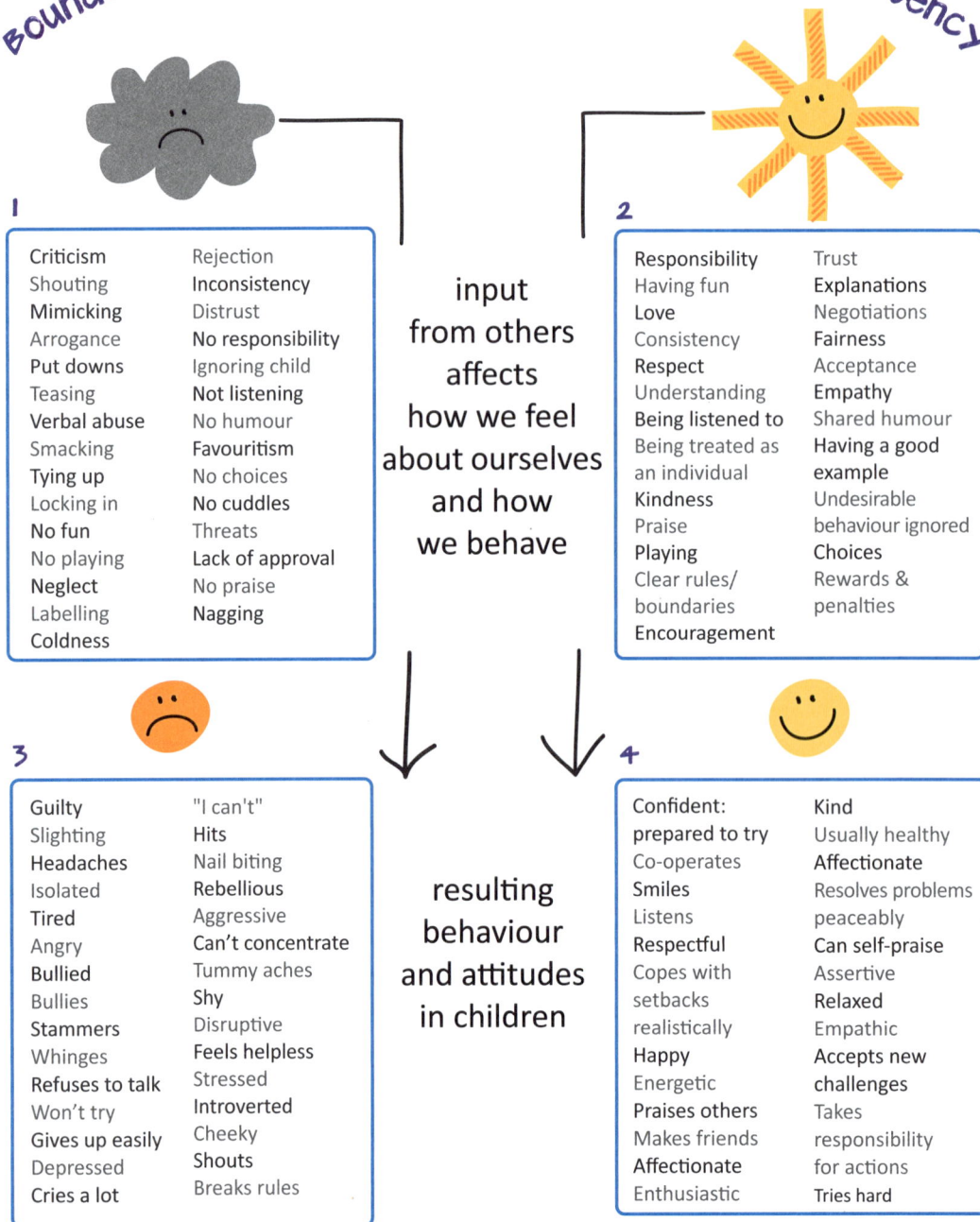

input
from others
affects
how we feel
about ourselves
and how
we behave

**1**

| | |
|---|---|
| Criticism | Rejection |
| Shouting | Inconsistency |
| Mimicking | Distrust |
| Arrogance | No responsibility |
| Put downs | Ignoring child |
| Teasing | Not listening |
| Verbal abuse | No humour |
| Smacking | Favouritism |
| Tying up | No choices |
| Locking in | No cuddles |
| No fun | Threats |
| No playing | Lack of approval |
| Neglect | No praise |
| Labelling | Nagging |
| Coldness | |

**2**

| | |
|---|---|
| Responsibility | Trust |
| Having fun | Explanations |
| Love | Negotiations |
| Consistency | Fairness |
| Respect | Acceptance |
| Understanding | Empathy |
| Being listened to | Shared humour |
| Being treated as | Having a good |
| an individual | example |
| Kindness | Undesirable |
| Praise | behaviour ignored |
| Playing | Choices |
| Clear rules/ | Rewards & |
| boundaries | penalties |
| Encouragement | |

resulting
behaviour
and attitudes
in children

**3**

| | |
|---|---|
| Guilty | "I can't" |
| Slighting | Hits |
| Headaches | Nail biting |
| Isolated | Rebellious |
| Tired | Aggressive |
| Angry | Can't concentrate |
| Bullied | Tummy aches |
| Bullies | Shy |
| Stammers | Disruptive |
| Whinges | Feels helpless |
| Refuses to talk | Stressed |
| Won't try | Introverted |
| Gives up easily | Cheeky |
| Depressed | Shouts |
| Cries a lot | Breaks rules |

**4**

| | |
|---|---|
| Confident: | Kind |
| prepared to try | Usually healthy |
| Co-operates | Affectionate |
| Smiles | Resolves problems |
| Listens | peaceably |
| Respectful | Can self-praise |
| Copes with | Assertive |
| setbacks | Relaxed |
| realistically | Empathic |
| Happy | Accepts new |
| Energetic | challenges |
| Praises others | Takes |
| Makes friends | responsibility |
| Affectionate | for actions |
| Enthusiastic | Tries hard |

## All behaviour has a reason - it's trying to meet a need

# The Challenge of Self-Esteem

Like plants, humans will struggle in a difficult climate and thrive in a nurturing one. Adults' attitudes and ways of behaving (top half of the chart) influence a child's attitudes, behaviour and self-esteem (bottom half of the chart). For children to have healthy self-esteem they need positive input from others around them – parents and carers, and also staff at school, other relatives, older siblings, etc. (Healthy self-esteem, which is positive, realistic and resilient, is not the same as big-headedness or a false self-esteem.)

All parents sometimes shout, feel fed up and snappy. All children are sometimes shy or aggressive or feel a bit low or hopeless. It's when this happens a lot that we need to pause and think about what might be going on. Children are all born different, too: some are naturally more easy-going than others. As parents, we find it easier on some days than others to be patient, to listen, to take an interest in what our children are doing. It is much harder if the weather is stormy in our own lives and we are unhappy or stressed.

As parents we may feel angry or sad if we see our own childhoods reflected in the left-hand side of the chart. We may feel accused, resentful or ashamed if we see our own children's behaviour reflected in box 3, and realise that we may be playing a part in it. These feelings are quite common. Even if our families have a tendency to repeat the pattern on the stormy side of the chart with each generation, things can be changed. And the person most likely to change it is YOU. Just by reading this book, thinking about your relationship with your child, perhaps joining a parenting group, you have begun to change the emotional climate for your family.

Everything you do to shift yourself over to the sunny side will help your children to shift too. It will help them to stay on the sunny side if they become parents, making it easier for their children to do the same - the pattern can be repeated down the generations in a healthier way. And it will be you who started this happening. You are the person in the narrow neck of the sand timer, with the courage to change; you deserve to feel proud of yourself.

If your family is already in the sunny side of the chart most of the time you may feel grateful for your own happy childhood or for the support you have from your partner or family. However bringing up children is the hardest job we do, so even with good experiences and support we still deserve to appreciate ourselves for what we're doing well.

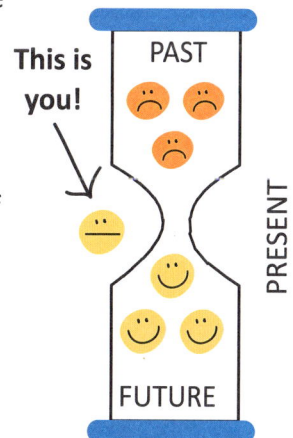

# choices and consequences

We all want to feel that we are in charge of our own lives. We want to be "driving our own bus" rather than being a helpless passenger hiding in the back! This is where our sense of personal power comes in, and as we've already seen, it's linked to self-esteem. The ability to make thoughtful choices for ourselves is the third part of the triangle.

It is helpful for children gradually to learn to make choices, and to discover what happens as a result of the choices they make – what the consequences are. If they aren't given the chance to learn this, they may grow up knowing only how to do as they're told, which is not much help in adult life. Or they will make choices without even realising they are, and fail to take responsibility for them.

If children are given no choice, they will feel powerless, which usually brings with it a host of other difficult feelings – and results in hard-to-handle behaviour.

The choices we give children range from deciding between an apple and a banana, to which game they'd like you to play with them, to what subjects they want to study for GSCE. We need to strike a balance between giving no choice and giving too much. If, for example, we say to a three-year-old, "What would you like for tea?" he will probably say, "I don't know" – the choice is too wide. And if you have several older children and ask what they'd like, you'll get several different answers and that's making a rod for your own back.

One of the ways in which children need to learn about choice is that they have a choice about how they behave. This is an important life skill. Used well, giving Choices and Consequences keeps you in charge while the child keeps some power too. It ends the "Do as I say!" – "Shan't" stalemate. Using Choices and Consequences as part of a positive approach to discipline can reduce arguments and confrontations quite dramatically.

Don't you think children are spoilt nowadays because they have too much choice?

"Yes, sometimes that's true – and I agree it's not good for them. Adults need to be in charge of the choices, balancing respect for other people with the child's needs, and holding to the clear boundaries we thought about in Session 2."

# Giving children choices

We can offer children a choice many times during the day.

Giving children choices about how to behave is just the next step. Read on...

# steps for Giving Choices and consequences

**1**    Be clear and specific about the positive and negative choice of behaviour, and the positive and negative consequences that will follow

**2**    Relate the consequences to the behaviour

**3**    Choose consequences that mean something to the child

**4**    Use a calm, clear voice; threats, a threatening manner, ultimatums are counter-productive

**5**    Only give choices if it's right for the situation

**6**    Choose consequences you can keep to (without "punishing" yourself)

**7**    Give the child a few moments to reflect before asking for a decision

It can be tricky to know what behaviour we want. It can be equally hard to risk describing the behaviour you don't like, which is often how the child has already begun to behave. But you don't let it go on for ever. Whichever behaviour the child chooses next, you apply the consequence that matches it.

Things often seem harder in theory than they are in practice.

*Here's an example of Choices and Consequences:*

**Eden,** you have a choice.

You can either **help me tidy away the toys** or you can **leave me to do it.**

If you choose **to help me** then **we'll have time for an extra story.**

If you choose **not to help** then **we won't have time for the extra story.**

It's up to you – it's your choice.

Here's a chance for you to work out Choices and Consequences for yourself. Think of a situation that happens quite often between you and a child, one where you tend to end up saying, "Do as I tell you" and the child either says, "Shan't – you can't make me" or stomps off or starts crying but still doesn't co-operate. Keep it as simple and clear as you can.

When you've given it a try, check against the steps and against the example on the page opposite. There are some more cartoon examples on the next two pages to help you get the idea.

*Try using the language of 'positive' and 'negative' choices as shown below.*

# Practice sheet
## Giving choices and consequences

.................................... you have a choice.
*(child's name)*

You can either ...................................................................
*(positive behaviour choice)*

…or you can ...................................................................
*(negative behaviour choice)*

If you choose ...................................................................
*(positive behaviour choice)*

…then ...................................................................
*(positive consequence)*

If you choose ...................................................................
*(negative behaviour choice)*

…then ...................................................................
*(negative consequence)*

It's up to you - it's your choice.
*(It's crucial to finish by saying this)*

# Applying Choices and Consequences

It is so easy to get locked into conflict with children. Giving Choices and Consequences often (though of course not always – nothing works perfectly all the time!) makes conflicts melt away. And when children make a poor choice, they learn that they have to take the consequences.

## 😞 Instead of this

*Hey, you two. I've told you a thousand times to put things away. What a mess! Why do I always have to tidy up after you?*

## 😊 Give a choice

*Hey, you two. You have a choice. You can tidy up now or you can do it later. If you put things away now, you can watch TV before you go to bed. If you choose to do it later there won't be time for TV tonight. It's up to you.*

## 😞 Instead of this

*You get back here by 9 o'clock like I told you, or you'll be grounded for a week!*

## 😊 Give a choice

*We agreed you'd be back by 9 o'clock. If you keep to the time, you can go out again on Saturday night. If you're back late tonight, you'll have to stay in on Saturday. It's up to you – your choice.*

Using the formula for giving Choices and Consequences sometimes seems a bit long-winded, and it takes longer than laying down the law. But in the long term it's much quicker, because you don't spend so much time arguing and sorting out all the resentment that builds up when children feel powerless.

# Pitfalls in Giving Choices and Consequences

Here are two examples of Choices and Consequences that have gone wrong – and how to put them right.

### ☹ Instead of this

*You know one of our family rules is no fighting. You're always breaking the rules. I've had enough! Go to your bedrooms now!*

### ☺ Use Step 1

*Hey! One of our family rules is no fighting. You can take turns to use the remote, or you can fight over it. If you take turns you can go on watching TV; if you go on fighting, you'll both have to go to separate rooms.*

### ☹ Instead of this

*I'm fed up with you. You never look after your things. Look – your new scooter will be ruined in the rain! Put it away now or I'm taking it down to the tip tomorrow!*

*She doesn't mean it!*

### ☺ Use Steps 4 and 6

*You have a choice. Put your scooter away now or leave it to get wet. If you put it away you can ride it again tomorrow. If you leave it out, it will be locked in the shed for two days. You choose!*

*She means it!*

You might like to think of situations that often come up in your family, and try working out ways of dealing with them using Choices and Consequences. To avoid the pitfalls, use the steps and the practice sheet to guide you.

# REFLECTIONS

The words 'personal power' sound a bit weird, but I like the idea if it'll help the children to stop and think about what they're doing.

I think I've been feeling powerless all my life. It's hard to cope with the idea that I need to look after myself, and that I'm somehow allowing people to use me as a doormat.

My daughter's teacher says she'd do better in school if she had higher self-esteem. Now I understand what she's talking about, and what I can do to help boost it.

I feel gutted. I can see that I'm harsh with my children because that's what happened to me. But I feel so bad about it I really want to change.

We've said before that looking at how we bring up our children, and why, by thinking about what we learnt when we were young can be hard to do. It's especially true of this session. If you're feeling upset, try to recognise how brave you are even to be prepared to think about it, and to have old ideas challenged. It's not an easy thing to do.

It's a lot quicker to tell my son that if he doesn't do as I say he'll get punished, but maybe that's why he's so stroppy with me.

Quite often, the ideas in this session bring about an exciting breakthrough. When we can understand why children may be feeling bad about themselves, or powerless, or angry, or making foolish choices, it's easier to help them change – for their sakes and for our own.

# REFLECTIONS

**?** **What are you thinking and feeling at the end of the fourth session? If you would like to, record your own ideas here.**

..................................................................................................

..................................................................................................

..................................................................................................

..................................................................................................

# Time to Have a Go

SUN MON TUES WED THURS FRI SAT SUN MON TUES WED THURS FRI SAT

Play an extra game with the family.

Think about personal power, and how it links to self-esteem.

Notice how much choice you give your children and teenagers - too little, too much, about the right amount?

Practise giving Choices and Consequences. It's helpful to keep going with reinforcing family rules with rewards as well as penalties.

# Session 5:
## Feelings... and what we do with them, communicating clearly: Using "I" statements

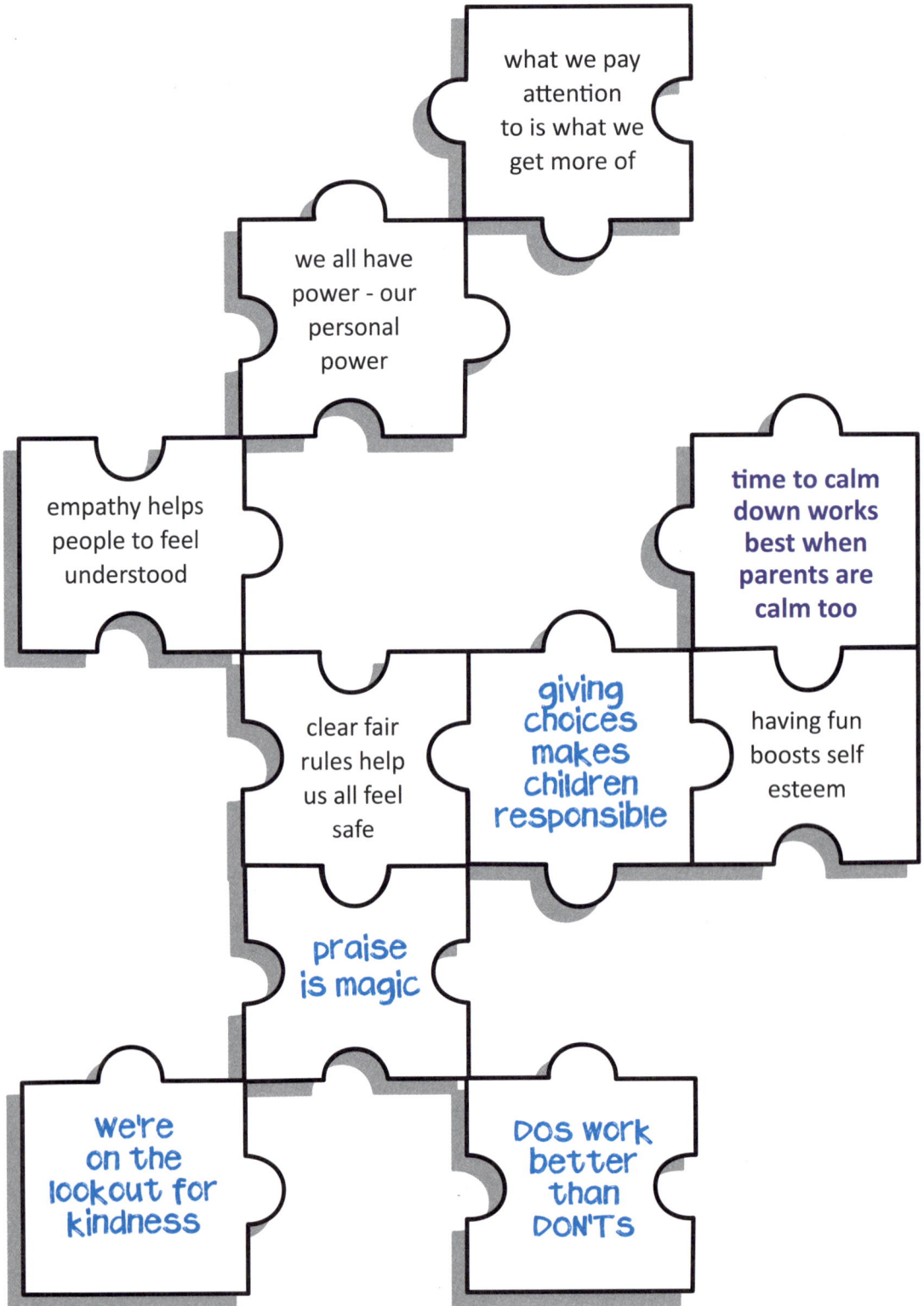

what we pay attention to is what we get more of

we all have power - our personal power

empathy helps people to feel understood

time to calm down works best when parents are calm too

clear fair rules help us all feel safe

giving choices makes children responsible

having fun boosts self esteem

praise is magic

we're on the lookout for kindness

DOS work better than DON'TS

# Feedback: What Parents Tell Us

**Family Rules**

"My daughter just said she didn't want either choice, so I said she had to choose one or I would choose for her."

**Giving Choices**

"I used to give my three-year-old too many choices, and she couldn't decide what she wanted. Now I just ask her to choose between two things, and she can cope with that."

**Giving Choices**

"I'm trying to let my son have more say- it's hard, but I've noticed that we have been arguing less than usual."

**Self-esteem**

"I'm beginning to see how everything links up. Noticing the good things and praising our children for them, thinking more about rewards than penalties, all helps their self-esteem- and mine gets a boost too because I'm feeling more positive about things."

**Choices and Consequences**

"I think I'm nagging less- and the kids have started to respond."

**?** **What have you tried so far, and how is it going? Make a note of how you're getting on if you'd like to.**

I had a go at...

and the result was...

# Feelings... and What We Do with Them

**The many ways we feel are an important part of us: we are emotional beings. As we grow up, we experience many different sensations that signify our emotions. We need to identify them, and learn how to cope with them.**

Some feelings are great: feeling happy, excited, contented, amused, calm, for example. Others are difficult or painful: fear, a sense of rejection, hate, jealousy are all hard to bear. We'd all rather have the enjoyable feelings than the painful ones. If we are upset and have to cope with feeling hurt, sad or angry, we can sometimes wish that we didn't feel at all. (When people are overwhelmed by their feelings, sometimes they do protect themselves by becoming emotionally numb. The trouble is that enjoyable feelings tend to get frozen as well as painful ones.)

Imagine what it would be like if you couldn't smell or taste. You wouldn't be able to tell the difference between food that is fresh, food that isn't pleasant, and food that's bad and will poison you. It's the same with feelings. They are like signposts: they tell us about safety and danger, trust and hurt, love and fear, desire and dislike. We need them all – even the unpleasant ones.

Children feel just as strongly as adults – perhaps even more, as they aren't so good at thinking about things. We can help them learn to understand their feelings, and to express them in helpful ways. Then they won't feel burdened by feelings they think they can't or shouldn't express. Of course, to help children learn how to do this, we need to be able to do it for ourselves. So it's helpful to be as self-aware as possible, and to develop our sensitivity towards others and what they are feeling – our empathy. These are two important building blocks in The Nurturing Programme – two of the Four Constructs (see page 18).

It's really hard for me to understand my feelings. Is that because my parents were British stiff-upper-lip types? I don't want my children to be like me.

"That's probably true. It's hard to learn to be at ease with how we feel if our parents haven't been able to help us. But we can be different – for ourselves and our children."

# Feelings, Feelings, Feelings!

**Here are some words to describe ways we feel. Which feelings are familiar? You could circle these.**

contented    encouraged    misunderstood    afraid    joy    stupid

fed up    bubbly    dull    wanted    stifled    ill at ease    loved    lonely

capable    generous    sad    positive    kind    mean

confused    angry    rejected    concerned    small

delighted    murderous    bewildered    proud    determined    bored

patient    pleased    relaxed

insecure    defensive    jealous    uncertain    calm

loving    interested    confident    independent

excluded    upset    worried    comfortable

rage    tearful    resentful

anxious    excited    respected    guilty    nervous    lethargic    depressed

unloved    amused    ecstatic    sexy    agitated    injustice    dishonest

paralysed    despairing    embarrassed    aggressive

happy    cheerful    curious    interested    powerless

annoyed    rebellious    helpless    trusting

irritated    hostile    inferior    powerful    relieved    responsible

shy    helpful    stressed    disappointed

safe    valued    hurt    understood    suspicious    friendly

inadequate    furious    assertive    miserable

blamed    frustrated    discouraged    glad

**Can you think of others that haven't been included? You will probably think of plenty more, as there are literally hundreds of words for feelings. Add your extra ones to the page.**

# Responding with Empathy

There are different ways of reacting to someone else's feelings, some more helpful than others. Honestly describing our own feelings, and being as sensitive as we can in suggesting what we think our children may be feeling, helps them to identify the sensations in their bodies connected to different feelings, and to learn the right words for them. An understanding, empathic response from someone else always feels good, however old we are.

## Unhelpful

*Stop scowling, and go and find something to play with while I feed the baby. It's bad to be jealous.*

## Helpful

*My guess is that you're feeling left out. That's hard, isn't it? Shall I tell you a story while I feed the baby?*

## Unhelpful

*Mum, are you feeling sad?*

*No love, I'm just tired today.*

## Helpful

*Mum, are you feeling sad?*

*Yes love, I've just had some bad news and I'm feeling a bit sad.*

## Unhelpful

*Here's your lost teddy – now calm down and go to sleep.*

## Helpful

*Here's your lost teddy – I can see you're happy we've found him!*

# Troublesome Feelings

In our view, there are no "bad" feelings (though there are many painful ones). All feelings are OK, all feelings are valid. This challenges traditional social and religious views. Generations of boys, for example, have learned that they "shouldn't" feel upset, sad, shy or frightened. Similarly, girls were taught that to feel angry, to stand up for themselves, to be independent, wasn't allowed.

In different families, different feelings might cause problems. The important point is that many of us grow up believing some feelings are "good" and others "bad". But disapproval doesn't make the feelings go away. It just complicates them by adding guilt or fear or anger to what we were already feeling.

Strong feelings can lead to difficult behaviour. In trying to deal with the behaviour, it's easy to forget about the feelings that triggered it. To be emotionally healthy, it is important to acknowledge the distressing feelings rather than denying them; at the same time, we all need to learn how to manage our feelings so that we don't act out through hurtful or antisocial behaviour. It is understandable that a toddler feels jealous of a new baby brother; it isn't OK to throw the baby out of the window. If a man's wife leaves him for another man, he may well feel rejected, angry, full of hate; it isn't OK to murder the wife or the lover.

**?** **What feelings met with disapproval or got you into trouble as a child?** *(Think of teachers, friends, brothers and sisters as well as parents/carers.)* **Then ask yourself if you try to discourage any of your children's feelings. Make a note of your feelings, and theirs, if you'd like to.**

Feelings that got me into trouble when I was a child.........................

...........................................................................................................

Feelings I may try to switch off in my children.....................................

...........................................................................................................

**?** **The feelings our parents did not let us express are often the ones we block in our own children. Why?**

They may trigger the feeling in us – and we still feel anxious or guilty. Also, we want our children to be happy, and we can feel hurt or believe we are failing if they show unhappy or "negative" feelings. Learning to manage and safely express our own feelings is a great way to use our personal power, and a real help to our children.

# What We Do With Difficult Feelings

Emotions we find difficult or painful can be hard to manage. Here are some ways we deal with them. Which are your preferred ones?

The swirl image in each drawing represents our feelings.

## Suppressing

Locking our feelings away, burying them, removing them from our conscious awareness.

## Bottling Up

Holding the feelings inside us; we may become so pressurised we eventually explode.

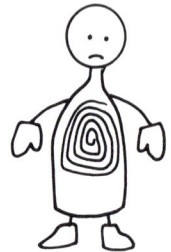

## Withdrawing

Hiding away; we may become depressed, or feel paralysed or helpless.

## Dumping

Blaming others for the way we feel; handing over responsibility for our feelings to others.

## Acting Out

Being taken over by the feelings, often losing control altogether - yelling, being violent.

All the ways of dealing with painful feelings pictured on the last page may seem to help at the time, but they don't actually solve the problem – either for us as individuals or in our relationships with other people. They all tend to be destructive.

*Here are some more constructive alternatives to think about.*

## Reflecting

Accepting our feelings without being overwhelmed by them, thinking about them, reframing and resolving them

## Expressing

Letting the feelings out: acknowledging them to ourselves
(e.g. crying or talking to someone)

## Letting go

When we have taken notice of the messages our feelings bring, we can release them.

It's a good idea to find as many ways as we can to help us recover from difficult feelings. If we have no way of letting them go, they can pile up until they're like a big heavy sack we have to carry around with us. This not only feels awful, but is bad for our health, too.

There's an exercise at the end of this session to help us let go of our difficult feelings when we feel ready to release them.

# Feelings Quiz

One way of getting to know and understand our feelings better is to notice what situations and events trigger certain emotions in us. Here are some common feelings – can you think of times you experience these? When we're aware of what gives us feelings we enjoy, we can try to find more of those experiences – and perhaps to think about how to deal with ones that are uncomfortable for us.

I feel happy when...

I feel resentful when...

I feel generous when...

I feel excited when...

I feel angry when...

I feel sad when...

I feel powerless when...

I feel valued when...

I feel loved when...

I feel depressed when...

I feel proud when...

I feel satisfied when...

I feel scared when...

I feel frustrated when...

I feel embarrassed when...

I feel hurt when...

I feel stressed when...

I feel calm when...

I feel stupid when...

I feel confident when...

I feel helpless when...

I feel respected when...

# Handling Anger

Anger can be one of the most powerful and difficult emotions. It arises when we feel threatened. The feeling of anger is often the result of other feelings – a reaction to fear or hurt of some kind. It is part of a protective "fight or flight" reaction, a survival instinct we share with animals.

When we feel threatened or see someone else in danger we have a surge of the hormone adrenaline in our bodies. This prepares us for "fight or flight"; you can imagine being faced with a roaring tiger and needing to do one or the other! The sense of threat we experience is often emotional as much as physical. If we don't find safe ways to express or manage the feeling it may be turned towards others in violence or aggression or turned inwards and increase our risk of depression. Children who have experienced frequent threat or witnessed violence will be hypersensitive to the feeling and will need greater adult help to calm themselves.

We may become aware of anger building up gradually, or we may suddenly be overwhelmed by it. Usually it's possible, if we think back carefully, to track events that have provoked other feelings (anxiety, frustration, tension, for example) that combine to produce the angry reaction.

If we often feel angry in situations that, when we have calmed down, we can see are not all that dangerous, it's a sign that we have a backlog of old, unexpressed feelings waiting to be released. We may need help in letting go of them; it can be hard to do this on our own. Many people find it helps to have the support of a relaxed, confident and kind listener – a wise friend or someone trained to help others, such as a counsellor.

Expressing feelings can be the first step in recovering from them. It allows us, in a calmer frame of mind, to move on to thinking about the situation that provoked those feelings, and what if anything we need to do either about the situation itself or about our response to it. In other words, expressing our feelings is a means to an end, not an end in itself. This is true of all difficult feelings, not just anger.

It's helpful if we can learn to express our anger safely – and to teach our children to do this too. Try noting down on the next page your own responses to feeling angry. Then turn to page 122 to compare your ideas with those of other parents. In the groups we compare our ideas in 1 and 4 and often laugh as we realise that we expect children to deal with their anger in much calmer ways than we do ourselves. What kind of role models are we?

# Responses to Anger

**Complete these statements with as many examples as you can:**

When I am angry I respond by: .............................................................
...........................................................................................
...........................................................................................

When I am angry I also feel: .............................................................
...........................................................................................
...........................................................................................

...and others around me seem to feel .............................................
...........................................................................................
...........................................................................................

When I was a child and someone was angry, I remember feeling:
...........................................................................................
...........................................................................................

Ways we would like children to deal with their anger: ....................
...........................................................................................
...........................................................................................
...........................................................................................

# Responses to Anger

**Responses from other parents:**

## When I am angry I respond by:

*shouting, lashing out, withdrawing, saying horrible things, sulking, nagging, going icy cold, exploding, throwing/breaking things, counting to ten, going away, swearing, bursting into tears, playing music very loud*

## When I am angry I also feel:

*crazy, lonely, misunderstood, upset, wound up, I want to be alone, like thumping someone, depressed, unlovable, stupid, powerful, frightened, guilty, motivated, like running away*

## ... and others around me seem to feel:

*threatened, shut out, helpless, "here we go again", frightened, bewildered, angry back, like running away, anxious, impatient, defensive*

## When I was a child and someone was angry, I remember feeling:

*frightened, guilty, paralysed, rebellious, relieved (especially if they were angry with someone else for a change), over-protective, insecure, worried, angry, sympathetic, like hiding or running away, tearful, desperate*

## Ways we would like children to deal with their anger:

*control it, count to ten, walk away, talk about it calmly, not be angry (!), be reasonable, explain why they're angry, go away until they've calmed down, apologise*

# Safe Ways to Deal with Angry Feelings

We can learn to recognise our own build-up of anger. It's then sometimes possible to take action before we reach our flashpoint, and to prevent the explosion. If it's too late, we can help ourselves to recover. Different things are possible in different situations, and work for different people. Use your personal power in a positive way to find out what works for you, and help your family to do the same.

**?** **What triggers your anger? Note down your own flashpoints.**

**?** **Then, from the list below - and with any additions that work for you - make a note of how you can help yourself both before you reach explosion point, and afterwards**

My anger flashpoints

............................................................................................................

............................................................................................................

What I can do before I explode... ..................................................................

............................................................................................................

............................................................................................................

What I can do after I've blown it... .................................................................

............................................................................................................

## Anger without Danger

*have a cool drink ... go for a walk ... stroke an animal ... practise slow, calm breathing while counting to ten (or a hundred) ... track back the events/feelings leading up to feeling angry ... think of something funny ... do something kind for someone ... relax in a hot bath ... draw a picture ... do something energetic (go for a run ... dig the garden ... clean the house) ... dance energetically ... talk about it with someone supportive ... knead dough (clay or playdoh for children) ... say "I feel angry because..." out loud ... play/listen to music ... out of earshot of others, scream loudly ... "write out" the anger ... take Time to Calm Down alone ... do relaxation exercises*

# Communicating Clearly: Using "I" Statements

**If we want other people to respect us and understand us, we need to communicate clearly.**

When we don't like a situation, we may grumble and moan. We use blaming "You" messages, such as: "You're making so much noise you're giving me a headache", or "You make me so angry – it's your fault I crashed the car!" This is a bit like a child saying, "He made me do it!", and it doesn't usually work very well. We can probably all think of times when we have been blamed and criticised by someone, and remember how unpleasant it felt. None of us reacts well to blame; we often feel threatened and lash out.

Alternatively we may pretend to ourselves that it doesn't really matter. Later we may notice that we're feeling resentful or irritable. This doesn't solve things either. If the problem continues, we're likely to feel more resentful still, until we explode in anger or subside into depression. Things can go from bad to worse...

"I" statements give us a way of talking about difficult situations, thoughts and feelings that helps us understand one another better, and reduces the number of destructive arguments we have.

When we use an "I" statement, we're expressing our feelings, thoughts and needs – and taking responsibility for them. Although this may feel risky, it increases our chances of being understood. We still can't be sure that the other person will respond the way we'd like them to, but it's more likely than if we sulk or moan or lose our temper. People aren't mind-readers – we have to be clear in our own minds about what's going on, and then tell others our point of view.

My teenagers are always complaining, especially if I ask them to help with chores. They make me feel bad when they grumble about everything. What can I do?

"It sounds as though you and they might all be more used to "You" messages. Maybe if you start using "I" statements, they'll pick up the idea and learn to be clearer with you about their problems."

# Responding to Challenge

Let's think about how we respond when someone challenges or confronts us. We tend to respond in one of four ways.

| Submissive | Passive Aggressive | Aggressive | Assertive |
|:---:|:---:|:---:|:---:|
| ↓ | ↓ | ↓ | ↓ |
| yielding | manipulative | blaming "YOU" messages | "I" statements |
| ↓ | ↓ | ↓ | ↓ |
| powerless/resentful | power struggle | power struggle | power retained |
| Increased STRESS | Increased STRESS | Increased STRESS | Reduced stress |

When we are assertive, it's like being balanced on a seesaw. We keep our sense of power, and the other person does too. We both respect the other's point of view, and manage to resolve the issue. It's often what is known as a win–win situation: we both feel OK afterwards, and the relationship becomes stronger.

Being submissive, passive aggressive or aggressive usually unbalances the seesaw of a relationship. If we give in when we don't want to, we may wake up in the middle of the night and find we're angry or miserable. We may get pushed around again another time – or take it out on someone weaker. If we respond aggressively, the problem usually escalates unless the other person becomes submissive, in which case we may feel we've "won". But the other person will feel worse, and our relationship with them will worsen too.

We may always respond in the same way, but often our reaction depends on the power relationship between the other person and ourselves. Some people are submissive with those in authority (like a boss), and aggressive towards those with less power than themselves (such as children). Others become aggressive when confronted by an authority figure, and are calmly assertive in other situations. Most of us use a mixture of all four responses, depending on our mood and that of the other person. Using an "I" statement is a good way of being assertive – of balancing the seesaw of our relationships.

# Using "I" Statements

Do you remember the parent's question about her complaining teenagers at the beginning of this section (see page 124)? Let's see how she might respond.

**If she is submissive**, she might say: "Oh dear, you're upset. Don't worry about the washing up – I'll do it again."

**If she is passive aggressive,** she might say: "Never mind. I'll do it" and then moan behind their backs or find other ways to get back at them.

**If she is aggressive**, she might say: "Don't start complaining again! You drive me crazy! And you're trying to get out of helping. So do the washing up and stop making a fuss."

**If she is assertive**, she might say: "I feel frustrated when I hear complaints about helping with household chores because it isn't reasonable for me to do everything. So what I'd like is for everyone to take their turn without making a fuss."

Let's look at some examples of how to turn "You" messages into "I" statements.

## ☹ "you" message

## ☺ "I" statement

## ☹ "you" message

## ☺ "I" statement

*To use "I" statements successfully, we need to:*

- say how we feel, using "feelings" words

- describe the situation without blaming or criticising the person involved - avoiding the word "you" keeps the description general, which is easier for the other person to hear

- be clear about why this is a problem for us - what need isn't being met

- think about what might help to solve the problem, from our point of view

When you're finding it difficult to be clear and say what you need to say without being over-apologetic or too tough, you may find an "I" statement helps you find your voice. Think of a situation that you'd like to deal with clearly and assertively. It could be a family issue, or something like returning faulty equipment to a shop.

*Here's a practice sheet to help you decide what you might want to say:*

# Practice sheet
## Giving an "I" statement

**I feel** *(say how you feel)* ..............................................................

**When** *(describe the situation and avoid using 'you')* ............................................

..........................................................................................

**Because** *(state your need that is not being met and why it matters)*

..........................................................................................

..........................................................................................

**What I'd like is** *(describe what would help you to meet your need)*

..........................................................................................

..........................................................................................

# Praise Power

We've thought a lot about feelings in this session, and about how we respond when we have difficult feelings. Let's end the session by thinking about ways we can boost our children's good feelings – and just as importantly, our own as well.

Here's a great way to end a child's day. At bedtime, talk briefly about all the good things that have happened during the day. Don't mention any bad moments. Just focus your attention on what the child has coped with well, what you're pleased with them about, what they have enjoyed. It's a chance to boost self-esteem with praise and encouragement, and help the child go to sleep feeling happy and relaxed.

**Remember praise for being? If you've had a hard day and can't think of much to praise, it can come to your rescue. And even on the easier days it's wonderful to give some praise for being, too.**

## Reward Charts

Some parents like to have a bedtime reward chart that the child can fill in during these few minutes as a reminder of what's gone particularly well during the day.

Here are some examples to get you started. Don't worry if you're short of ideas or don't think you're artistic. Children don't expect our efforts to be perfect; they will usually come up with great ideas of their own, and enjoy designing them too.

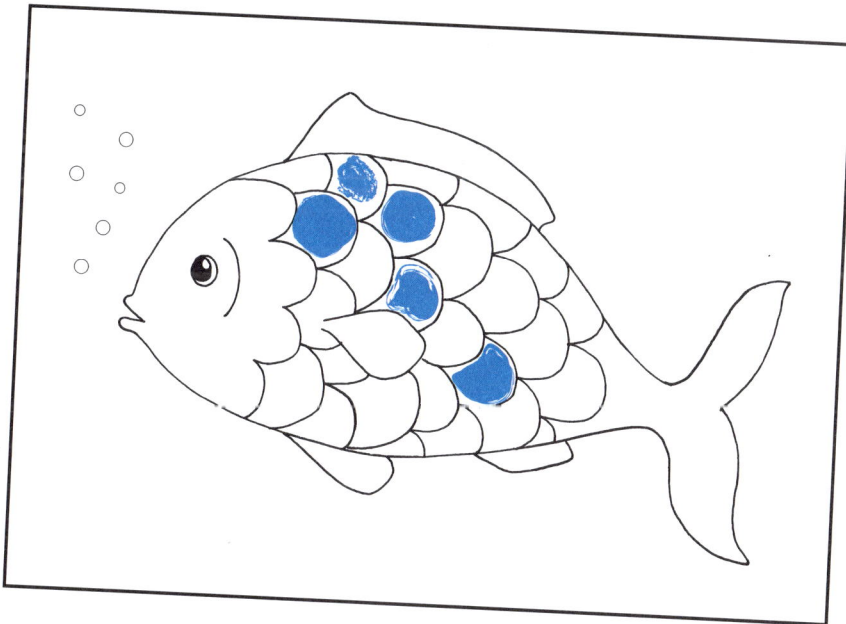

# Praise Power Boost for ourselves

We are thinking a lot about helping our children feel good about themselves. Some of us won't have been helped us do this when we were children. This makes it hard to help our children, and can leave us feeling bad about ourselves.

> **?** **Do you often give yourself a hard time when things go badly?**
> **Do you ever find yourself thinking, "I did that well!"**

Many adults find it easier to be self-critical than to focus on our good points. This is likely to be because we heard more critical comments when we were young, so they feel normal. Praise from others may feel strange if it's new for us; the idea that we might pat ourselves on the back, to notice what we're doing well, or pause to think about the day and enjoy what we've achieved or how we've coped can seem even more weird.

It's almost as if we have a recording in our heads that gets played over and over again, reminding us of all our faults. But criticism just makes us feel bad, and we can make ourselves feel worse by listening to this. We can gradually silence the old destructive comments by replacing them with more positive ones. We can learn to take pride in ourselves.

> **?** **In Session 1 we thought about praising ourselves as well as others.**
> **Four sessions on, does it seem any easier to spot your good points?**

Remembering to take pride in ourselves is easier if we begin by doing it at the same time each day. To remind you, you could put a note on the bathroom mirror saying, "Have I patted myself on the back today?" If you'd like to record when you give yourself a Praise Power boost, at bedtime or any other time of day, here's a chart to get you started. The idea is to draw a hand in the space every day you pat yourself on the back.

| Mon | Tues | Wed | Thurs | Fri | Sat | Sun |
|-----|------|-----|-------|-----|-----|-----|
|     |      |     |       |     |     |     |
|     |      |     |       |     |     |     |

# Releasing Feelings: the Hot Air Balloon

Here is a way to let go of difficult feelings. You could read it for yourself, ask someone to read it to you, or record it on tape. Go through it slowly, pausing to let the images and sensations build up in your mind.

Start to relax by taking some slow, easy breaths and now begin to picture a brightly coloured hot air balloon, hovering ready to lift its basket off the ground and up into the sky.

When the balloon and the basket are clear in your mind, take your troublesome feelings and put them into the basket. Let them take up as much space as they need; there's plenty of room.

Now picture the balloon slowly lifting the basket off the ground... gradually it rises up and up until it is outlined against the clear blue sky... keep watching as it rises into the air, getting higher and higher, until it begins to seem smaller as the breeze blows it gently away from you, carrying away the troublesome feelings.

Where those old feelings were inside you, imagine a new sense of lightness, or space, or peace... and as you watch the balloon drift away until it is only a speck in the distance and becomes part of the blue sky, let yourself be filled with this lightness, space, peace...

Then, when you're ready, wiggle your fingers and toes and come back to the room.

# REFLECTIONS

It's helpful to remember that feelings drive the way everyone behaves, it makes so much fall into place.

It's never struck me before that there are other feelings behind the angry way my children behave. Maybe if I can tune in earlier they won't explode so often.

I get tongue-tied when I want to tell someone I don't like what's happening; I bottle it up and then lose my temper over some silly little thing. I'm going to try working out some "I" statements instead.

I don't think I know what I'm feeling half the time. No wonder the kids' strong feelings are hard for me to understand.

I'm not sure about all this talk of emotions. I'd always thought it's better to forget about them, but it's true that they don't really go away.

So many of us have grown up without much attention being paid to how we feel. This session can come either as a welcome eye-opener or as a daunting challenge. If nobody's ever helped us with our feelings, how can we be aware of them and deal with them — let alone be sensitive to other people! Well, we can — it's never too late to start thinking more about it.

The more we are aware of our feelings, the better we manage and express them healthily, the more our children will be able to do the same. And the more we can tune in to their feelings — the more empathic we are — the more tuned in to others they will become too. Without realising it, they will copy us. And as being "emotionally literate" helps all relationships, we'll all be better off.

# REFLECTIONS

**?** **What are you thinking and feeling at the end of the fifth session? If you would like to, record your own ideas here.**

............................................................

............................................................

............................................................

# Time to Have a Go

SUN   MON   TUES   WED   THURS   FRI   SAT   SUN   MON   TUES   WED   THURS   FRI   SAT

Notice your feelings, and try to sense how others in the family may be feeling too.

Read the Misery-making beliefs and better choices chart (page 134). Is there a new way you could approach a difficult feeling or unhelpful belief about yourself?

Practise using "I" statements rather than blaming others with "You" messages.

Give Praise Power at bedtime, and praise yourself too.

Fill in the Family Log (see page 135).

## 🙁 Misery-making beliefs

1 *I must always please my family, my friends and neighbours, no matter how busy or tired I am.*

2 *My children must behave perfectly all the time. If they don't, it proves that I am a very bad parent, and deserve to be blamed for it.*

3 *When things go wrong, it must be my fault, and it is truly catastrophic. I am responsible for everything that happens to me and my family.*

4 *My child is already so bad that there is nothing I can do to make anything better in the family.*

5 *I must solve any problem I have at once, or it will prove that nothing will ever make any difference – that the situation is hopeless.*

6 *I must feel warm and loving towards my children at all times or I am a bad parent and a bad person.*

7 *My house must always be perfectly clean and tidy. If it isn't, I am useless and should be ashamed of myself.*

8 *If I am unhappy or tense, either I or someone else are to blame, and I should be very angry about it.*

9 *There is a perfect solution to every situation, and if I can't find it I am a complete failure.*

10 *I'm completely selfish to have any needs of my own.*

## 🙂 Better choices

1 *I will do my best with my children and myself; if others sometimes don't like it, that is their business, not mine.*

2 *I don't depend on my children or their perfection for my own sense of worth. I will do my best to teach them how to behave well, but no child is perfect and it's OK for us to make mistakes.*

3 *It's hard when things go wrong. I will do what I can to see that they don't go wrong again in the same way, but there are some things that I cannot change and are not my responsibility.*

4 *The way my child behaves always has a reason, and I can influence it by trying to understand and changing the way I handle him/her and myself.*

5 *I will make one small change at a time, and will try to remember that it usually takes a while before any change can be noticed.*

6 *I can feel however I want to feel, but I am responsible for not hurting my children whether or not I feel warm and loving towards them.*

7 *People are more important than houses, and that includes me.*

8 *I can honour and accept responsibility for my own feelings, and don't have to blame anyone for them.*

9 *There's no single right answer. I'll try lots of different solutions until I find one that works in this situation.*

10 *I have needs too, and I can try to meet my own as well as other people's.*

Misery-making beliefs don't help us. We feel powerless, and tend to give ourselves a hard time. It is helpful to try and find another way of looking at things.

# Taking stock

This is the halfway point in The Nurturing Programme's 10-week Parent Programme. It's a good time to stop and think about what's happening in the family. Have you noticed any changes? Things may well be improving; it's also possible that when we begin to change, children may feel suspicious or confused, and things may temporarily appear to be getting worse! Please make a note of how things are going. If you are coming to a group, you might like to copy here what you write on your Family Log sheet.

## Family Log

How am I changing? ..........................................................................................

..........................................................................................................................

How do I think the family is changing? ........................................................

..........................................................................................................................

What do the family say is better? .................................................................

..........................................................................................................................

What ideas and strategies am I using confidently? ....................................

..........................................................................................................................

Which ones would I like to feel more confident about? ........................

..........................................................................................................................

What is the emotional temperature in the family?

*(Mark the thermometer for the whole family, and for individuals if you'd like to.)*

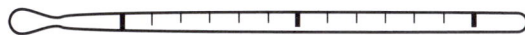

| cold | warm | hot |
|------|------|-----|
| critical | nurturing | angry |
| uptight | kind | shouting |
| contempt | respectful | critical |
| distant | fun | fighting |

# Session 6:
# Kinds of Touch and Nurturing Ourselves

what we pay attention to is what we get more of

be assertive - use "I" statements

we all have power - our personal power

empathy helps people to feel understood

time to calm down works best when parents are calm too

clear fair rules help us all feel safe

giving choices makes children responsible

having fun boosts self esteem

praise is magic

feelings are signposts

we're on the lookout for kindness

DOS work better than DON'TS

# Feedback: What Parents Tell Us

### "I" Statements

"I tried with a really difficult thing that's going on at work, and messed it up. I think I need to get it right with easier things first."

### Family Log

"My older daughter used to be the difficult one. She's easier to deal with now- but my younger daughter's playing up. I think she wants more attention! I asked the children; they say I'm shouting less. I think they're fighting less, too."

### Praise Power

"It's magic. My son never used to stay in bed after I'd said goodnight. He's so happy with our Praise Power moments at bedtime he settles down straight away."

### Misery-making beliefs

"It felt as though they all applied to me at times. I keep re-reading the 'better choices' part to try and convince myself that I can record over all those old messages."

### "I" Statements

"It's helpful having a formula I can rehearse before I go and deal with a situation."

**?** **What have you tried so far, and how is it going?**
**Make a note of how you're getting on if you'd like to.**

I had a go at...

and the result was...

# Kinds of Touch

**Touch is one of the most powerful ways we communicate with each other. Babies respond to it from the moment they are born.**

The way we touch tells another person how we feel towards them, and children are particularly good at sensing this. Many of us have memories of gentle, nurturing touch that showed love, kindness, trust, and brought comfort when we were hurt. For others, our memories include painful, frightening touch. In this session we think about different kinds of touch, and how they affect us.

One kind of touch familiar to many children all over the world and throughout history is punishing touch – touch that is meant to hurt. In some families this has been the usual way of disciplining children for generations. Nowadays it is a hotly debated question. Some people are relieved that at last things are changing; for others it can be unsettling when the practice of punishing children by smacking or hitting them is questioned. The Nurturing Programme view is that physical punishment doesn't work in the long term, and isn't helpful to the child or to family relationships.

I feel awful when I hit my child. Are you saying that all these other ideas we're thinking about mean I won't need to smack him to get him to behave?

"Yes. Most of us smack children when we're at the end of our tether. Positive discipline helps us manage our children without getting to the point where we lose control, so smacking becomes redundant."

I find it hard to cuddle my children as I never had any gentle touch. Will it harm them if I can't do it?

"You can find other ways of showing children affection if touch is difficult: warm smiles touch with a look; praise touches with words. A pat on the shoulder and other types of touch might be OK for you."

*Here are examples that parents come up with of the three main kinds of touch.*

# Kinds of Touch

| Nurturing touch | | Hurting touch | Scary touch |
|---|---|---|---|
| **OK** | | **not OK** | |
| holding hands | cuts | smacking | threats of hurting touch |
| linked arms | scrapes | hitting | any touch from someone I don't like or trust |
| hugs | dentist | pinching | |
| cuddles | sports injuries | hair-pulling | |
| OK tickling | accidental injuries | boxing ears | unwanted sexual touch |
| back rubs | | grabbing | |
| massage | injections | rape | excessive tickling |
| welcome sexual touch between adults | childbirth (for many) operations | kicking | |
| | | arm-twisting | unwanted hugs, kisses, etc. |
| kissing | **Extra ideas:** | **Extra ideas:** | |
| stroking | | | threatening looks/gestures |
| arm around shoulders | | | |
| | | | **Extra ideas:** |
| **Extra ideas:** | | | |

**? How do you react when you look at this list?**

For some people it can be painful even to see the words and remember some of their past experiences. If this is true for you, go slowly in this section, and stop if you need to take a break.

# Kinds of Touch

## Nurturing touch

is touch that sends messages of love and affection, and brings us closer to people.

## Ok-hurting touch

there are two kinds of hurting touch. Some touch is painful but in a way it feels OK because we know it is either an accident or is meant to help us.

## Not-OK hurting touch

on the other hand, Not-OK touch that is intended to hurt – is punishing touch. Because of this, it carries emotional as well as physical pain.

## Scary touch

this may not actually hurt (though much hurting touch is also frightening), but it feels threatening or unsafe. Nurturing touch can become scary if it's unwanted.

We can give an alternative to nurturing touch with kind looks and words. We can also inflict hurt with harsh looks and words. The old saying, "Sticks and stones may break my bones, but words can never hurt me" is nonsense. Long after physical bruises have faded, we may remember the hurtful things people say to us.

## Why Adults Hit Children

Many children experience some form of physical punishment while they are growing up – it's still very common. There are various reasons why it is used. For a long time, hurting touch has been used as a way of telling children that adults are angry with them. Children who grow up with the message, "When you're a grown-up, you can hit people if you're angry" may become violent adults, or may become victims of others' violence. In Session 5 we looked at different ways of managing anger.

**?** **Isn't it more helpful to show children non-violent ways of expressing anger so they don't get into fights?**

Some people think that punishing children in this way is useful for teaching them the difference between right and wrong. We'll do an activity that will test this theory.

Many parents resort to smacking because they do not know what else to do. Without physical punishment, they have no way of showing their displeasure at the child's behaviour. The suggestion that it's better not to hit children leaves them feeling powerless – and afraid that their children will be out of control. Think back to Session 4 and the feelings that go with a lack of power; it's understandable that we lash out when we're feeling powerless – we may also be feeling frustrated or frightened, and worried that the children are beyond our control or in danger.

Learning to use other ways of disciplining children, rewarding their good behaviour and penalising poor behaviour, can take the pressure off parents as well as children. Let's see what we learned from the hurting touch we experienced when we were children.

**?** **If you prefer, just think about the statements on the notepad – you don't need to write down your responses if you would rather keep them private.**

Think back to when you were a child, and remember how you felt at the time about hurting touch – not just from parents or carers, but from teachers, older siblings, grandparents, etc. as well. If you were never hit, or can't remember, imagine how you might have felt. To compare your ideas with those of other parents, turn to the completed chart (page 146). You may like to add to your lists any extras from it that are true for you.

## When I was hit as a child...

I felt:

and I learnt:

and I felt towards the person who hit me:

When we do this exercise in the groups, it turns out that for almost everyone the experience of hurting touch was painful in an unhelpful way. It produced fear or anger or hate or rebelliousness or deceit or mistrust – hardly the ingredients for a good relationship. While we remember the adult's anger, we often can't remember what we were punished for or what we'd done wrong. We just remember that they hurt us. If it is very painful for you to remember your childhood experiences and the feelings they bring up, take a break before reading on if you need one.

# Why We Use Hurting Touch

**It is worth asking ourselves what we as parents hope to achieve when we use hurting touch to punish children, and how we feel about it. What are your aims?**

On the page opposite is an exercise to help you work this out, and further suggestions for reflection. Complete the exercises first, and then read on.

We have the best intentions when we punish our children: we want them to learn how to behave, to learn right from wrong, to know when what they do is not acceptable. One reason why punishing touch is still used is that it's been around for so long, and the myths about it run deep in all of us.

**? Did anyone ever find out the child's point of view?**

Our reasons for punishing children – wanting them to respect us, to know that we are in charge, to do as we say – are absolutely reasonable. When they don't do these things, it's not surprising that we feel frustrated and angry. It's these feelings that lead us to react violently, and most of us feel bad when we "lose it".

Sometimes we can feel powerful at first, because exploding with anger is a release. But the feeling doesn't last. None of us became parents wanting to feel angry, to lash out, to feel bad, to hurt our children. These feelings are unpleasant, and it's tough on us as well as on the children.

**Think about the times you punish your children – with actions or with harsh words. Then compare your ideas with those of others by turning to the completed chart, and add to your lists any extras from it if they are true for you.**

When I use hurting touch or wounding words with my children...

I want them to:

and I feel:

**?** **Some people say that smacking works, because it stops the behaviour. It can do – at the time. But is what the child learns, and how he or she feels, really helpful in the long run?**

In the groups we compare the first chart (our reactions when we were children) with the second chart (our intentions as adults). Are the children learning what we are hoping to teach them? You might like to compare them too. When parents discuss this after doing the exercises in a group, it's so clear that what we hope to achieve isn't really what happens – that what children learn is very different from what adults are trying to teach them.

**?** **In ten or twenty years' time, if our children were asked to complete the first chart, what might they have to say?**

Many parents feel troubled when they think about this. We would much rather have a good relationship with our children than a poor one, now and when they are grown up. As parents, we can choose between being builders and being demolition experts. Positive approaches to discipline help to meet our needs as parents to teach our children how to behave, and at the same time allow us to build a positive, healthy relationship with them.

# when I was hit as a child...

**I felt:**

horrible

unloved

sad

unwanted

blank

that I deserved it

resentful

terrified

angry

bad

belittled

desperate to escape

unjustly treated

hated

helpless

devastated

guilty

miserable

unsafe

needing revenge

**and I learnt:**

to pass on the blame

not to get caught

to switch off

that I wasn't loved

that nobody would listen to me

to do as I was told

I was useless

I was never good enough

to mind my own business

to be obedient

not to care

nothing at all

that grown-ups are unsafe

not to get close to people

to tell lies

to over-protect my younger siblings

it's all right for adults to hurt children

it's all right to hurt people you love

adults are dangerous

you solve arguments by using force

**and I felt towards the person who hit me:**

rage

disgust

hate

distrust

fear

respect

murderous

contempt

antagonistic

vengeful

loss of respect

scared

muddled

loathing

loss of confidence

loathing

sorry for making them angry

they were justified

afraid

defiant

# When I use hurting touch or wounding words with my children...

**I want them to:**

behave

understand

stop and think

give in

stop what they're doing

listen to me

stop nagging at me

treat me properly

know they're doing wrong

realise how angry I am

obey me

be sorry

pay attention

co-operate

do as they're told

shut up

take me seriously

be hurt

respect me

know I'm the boss

learn the difference between right and wrong

**and I feel:**

sorry

sick and ill

horrible

a failure

relieved

powerful

afraid of my anger

hurt

a bully

frustrated

awful

sad

justified

angry with myself

ashamed

relief, then guilty

out of control

like a fishwife

even angrier than before

disgusted with myself

useless – nothing works

loss of self-respect

# Time for a Breather

For some of us, thinking about unhappy times in our own childhood brings to the surface memories of some wounding experiences. The memories can provoke very strong, even overwhelming, feelings.

It can also be disturbing to realise that if we use hurting touch with our children, we may be inflicting on them some similarly wounding experiences. This may make us sad, bitter, angry, defeated – or many other feelings. If you are aware of having a strong reaction to the ideas and activities in this session, have a breather.

If the emotions feel overwhelming, you can use your five senses (sight, sound, smell, taste, touch) to help you. You may also want to confide in a friend. (If your emotions around these issues often feel unmanageable, you may decide to seek professional help.)

**Here are some ideas for ways of managing our strong feelings – and space for you to choose some of these or make a note of other ways that help you "come to your senses".**

## Coming to our senses

*light a candle and watch the flame ... smell some flowers ... eat a piece of fruit very slowly ... listen to birds singing ... stroke an animal ... have a hot bath, with scented bubbles ... cuddle a hot water bottle ... listen to soothing music ... watch clouds move across the sky ... hold a smooth stone in your hand and feel it get warm ... suck an ice cube*

I can help myself come to my senses by...

.......................................................................................................

.......................................................................................................

.......................................................................................................

.......................................................................................................

# Relaxation Holiday

One way we can help ourselves stay calm even when things are tough is to find a few moments to relax several times a day. This is one way of taking a short, relaxing break. You could read this for yourself or ask someone else to read it to you. Go through it slowly, pausing to let each sensation fill your mind.

**Sit comfortably, start with a few slow, easy breaths, and begin to relax and now let your mind create these sensations:**

Imagine the colours of the sky in a beautiful sunset...

Imagine the sound of water flowing in a stream...

Imagine the smell of a bonfire on a crisp autumn day...

Imagine the feel of smooth, clean sheets...

Imagine the sound of rain on the roof...

Imagine the smell of a field of grass in the hot summer sun...

Imagine the stars and moon in the dark sky on a clear night...

Imagine the taste of a favourite food...

Imagine the sound of a beautiful song...

Imagine the wind blowing on your face...

Imagine floating on the still water of a peaceful, shallow lake...

**Notice the feeling of calm and peace, and take time to enjoy it.**

Then, when you're ready, wiggle your fingers and toes and come back to the room. This is a lovely exercise to do with a child at bedtime, particularly if it has been a stressful day.

# Nurturing ourselves

**Parenting can be one of the most demanding jobs there is. To enjoy it, we need to think about our own well-being.**

When we are running a busy household, and perhaps going out to work as well, it can be hard to find a moment for ourselves. It's all too easy to put our needs at the end of the list – and as parents we never reach the end of the list!

**? What happens if we neglect ourselves?**

We may become exhausted, stressed, impatient, resentful about all the demands made on us, irritable and snappy, inconsistent, critical, forgetful... in this state of mind, it's hard to enjoy family life. Imagine yourself as a jug of water, and others in your family as glasses. If water from the jug is poured into each glass until the jug is empty, and it is not refilled, in the end everyone is worse off. We owe it to ourselves to fill ourselves up – and our families will benefit too.

We can be kind to ourselves in small, everyday ways. We can also be more conscious of the things we already do, but perhaps don't really notice are nurturing. We will enjoy these activities more if we deliberately give them as a gift to ourselves.

Looking after ourselves is not selfish, though many of us seem to think it is, and feel guilty if we take time for ourselves. Our needs are as valid as anyone else's. Some of us wait for others to meet all our needs, but we're likely to be in for a very long wait! Instead, it is a good use of our personal power to take matters into our own hands, and to make sure that every day we do something just for ourselves. If we're going to keep up our strength and resilience, we can't afford not to.

*I don't have a moment to myself most days. Where will I find the time to indulge myself?*

"It's hard but if we pause every now and then during the day, we have more energy to do what needs to be done – and we're not so tired and frazzled at the end of it."

*I don't have any money to spare, so how can I spend on myself?*

"We can give ourselves *time* – such as sitting down long enough to finish a cup of tea, or walking home through a park instead of along a busy road."

# The Nurturing Wheel

There are six areas of our lives that we need to nurture, and nurture in our children too. If you take the initial letter of each word on the Nurturing Wheel, you'll find they spell the word SPICES. And nurturing ourselves spices up our lives. It's best to do something regularly for ourselves in all six areas. If that seems impossible, we can start with just one, and gradually build up to more. Some activities cover more than one area; having supper with a friend and watching a good film together might be social, emotional, intellectual – and if you walk or cycle to the cinema, physical as well!

*Here are some examples in each of the six categories:*

**? What do you enjoy?**

## Physical
walking, sports, yoga, dancing, aerobics, gardening, massage

## Spiritual
enjoying beauty, appreciating nature, religion, meditation

## Intellectual
reading a magazine or book, listening to music or the radio, evening class

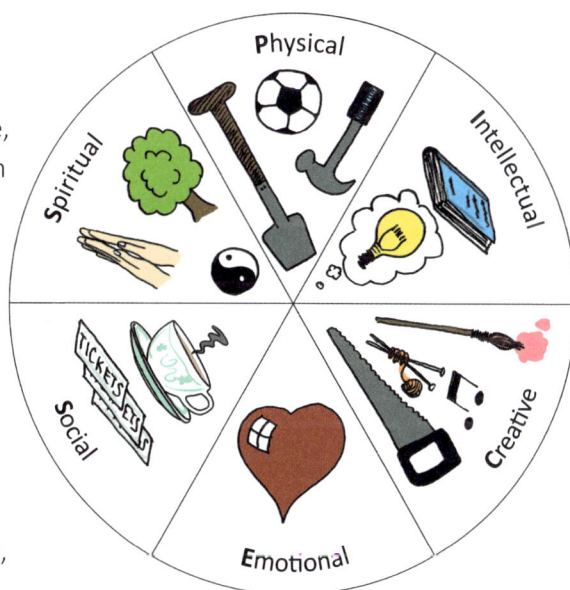

## Social
parties, phoning a friend, toddler club, days out, family outings

## Creative
making things, painting, writing making music

## Emotional
chatting with a good friend, hugs, laughing/crying, sharing/helping

We can nurture ourselves on our own, and in company. As our children grow up, they can learn that while we will often be available to meet their needs, sometimes we need time to meet our own as well. It is important for them to respect other people's needs, so by nurturing ourselves we are helping them too. We are also showing them that it is a good thing to do – so they won't grow up thinking it's selfish to look after themselves or feeling guilty when they do.

# Time for me

**?**  **How well do you nurture yourself, and how often?**
**Take a few moments to think about how you nurture yourself,**
**and write down your ideas as a reminder.**

What I do for myself now

| every day | once a week | sometimes |
| --- | --- | --- |
| | | |

What I'd like to do

| every day | once a week | sometimes |
| --- | --- | --- |
| | | |

What prevents me (practical difficulties and negative thoughts):

.......................................................................................................................

.......................................................................................................................

What I can tell myself instead:

.......................................................................................................................

.......................................................................................................................

# REFLECTIONS

No one can be calm and reasonable all the time. But I guess I won't feel so angry if I'm trying to look after myself and that includes not giving myself a hard time when I lose it.

I'd never realised that thinking about what I need would help the family as well as me. I'm going to start nurturing myself more.

I was lucky to have a happy childhood. This session has made me realise that when people blow up at their children it's probably because they've had a hard time.

It's been an eye-opener to find out what we all felt about the way we were punished. I want my children to have happy memories, and I'm determined to stop smacking from now on.

Sometimes people who have painful childhood memories have quite a strong reaction after this session, and find it hard to sleep or perhaps don't feel well. Others feel uncomfortable because we've highlighted the disadvantages of smacking and other forms of punishing touch. Whatever your reaction, we hope the session helps to explain why we think a positive approach to discipline is so much more helpful, for us as parents as well as for our children.

One way of helping ourselves when we have difficult feelings is to be kind to ourselves. Remind yourself that you have been doing the best you can, the best you knew how, even if that isn't necessarily the best there is. If we find it hard to treat our children gently, it's because we have not been treated gently ourselves. We can begin now to treat ourselves kindly by nurturing ourselves as well as others.

# REFLECTIONS

**?** **What are you thinking and feeling at the end of the sixth session? If you would like to, record your own ideas here.**

..................................................................................

..................................................................................

..................................................................................

..................................................................................

# Time to Have a Go

SUN MON TUES WED THURS FRI SAT SUN MON TUES WED THURS FRI SAT

Think about touch: your experience of it, and what your children are learning about it. What kind of gentle/ nurturing touch do you like to give and receive?

Nurture yourself in a new way.

Check through the Time to Have a Go ideas for earlier sessions, and see if there's anything more you'd like to do.

# Session 7:
# Ages and Stages in children's development and Helping children Grow Up

what we pay attention to is what we get more of

gentle touch is loving touch

be assertive - use "I" statements

we all have power - our personal power

empathy helps people to feel understood

time to calm down works best when parents are calm too

clear fair rules help us all feel safe

giving choices makes children responsible

having fun boosts self esteem

praise is magic

feelings are signposts

we're on the lookout for kindness

nurturing ourselves SPICES up our lives

DOS work better than DON'TS

# Feedback: What Parents Tell Us

### Thinking about touch

"It was the idea of everyone having a history of touch that got to me. I kept wondering what kind of touch history my children will have. That's helped me try not to smack them but to do more positive things instead."

### Nurturing Ourselves

"I don't often manage it yet, but when I do more for myself I notice I feel more like doing things for other people, too."

### Earlier Sessions

"I've realised that it's getting easier to remember to give praise, and to talk things through rather than flying off the handle. I'm calmer, and I think the family is as well."

### Thinking about touch

"I've noticed that we hardly touch each other in our house. I've tried touching my children a bit more - just a quick hug or a pat - and I think they like it."

**?** **What have you tried so far, and how is it going?**
**Make a note of how you're getting on if you'd like to.**

I had a go at...

and the result was...

# Ages and Stages in Children's Development

**Many of us worry about whether our children are developing "normally". It can be hard to know what is normal and what isn't.**

Children even in the same family develop at different rates in different ways, so when we've worked it out with a first child, the next one will still surprise us. We may tend to compare children, and become anxious if another child is doing "better" than ours.

Some children walk at seven months and can kick a football before they are two; others don't walk until they are a year old or more, and never seem to find the knack of connecting foot and ball. Some are fascinated by words, and learn to read before they go to school; others find it comes later. Some are sociable very early; others take much longer to make friends and enjoy being in a group. All this is "normal" development.

Children and teenagers have their own interests and abilities, and need to develop at their own pace. It helps if our expectations of them are a good "fit" with the child's own stage of development, whether it's tying shoelaces or learning to drive. A child who is able to do more than we allow will be frustrated, rebellious and difficult. A child who is expected to do more than he or she is ready for will probably be difficult too, and may feel inadequate.

Sometimes children do need extra help so if you're worried about your child speak with your health visitor, GP or your child's teacher.

**How can I tell if my expectations for the children are right for them?**

"Children themselves usually make it clear. If they're often bored or push us away a lot, they may need more challenges and responsibility. If they often seem clingy or overwhelmed, it's likely that we're expecting too much of them."

# Thinking about Expectations

Some people have parents who were very demanding, wanting us to lead a life mapped out by them. Some have parents who were supportive, offering guidance when we were young and helping us find our own way in life. Some parents seemed to have no expectations, and not to care much what we did. Most of us will have experienced a mixture of these attitudes.

It can be helpful to think about our parents' expectations and how we felt or feel about them – and to reflect on what we expect of our own children.

| Expectations my parents had of me | How I felt/feel about these |
|---|---|
| Unfair demands I may make on my child/children | How they may be feeling |

**?** **What occurs to you when you think about expectations, and compare your ideas with the examples we've given over the page?**

Sometimes we repeat our parents' attitudes – and if they were helpful, that's often fine. This doesn't always work. Children are not the same as us, so they may have surprising reactions, and ideas about obedience, independence, etc. change. If we found our parents' attitudes unhelpful, we may try to do the opposite with our children. This can work well, and can also go too far the other way.

You might like to refer back to boundaries, and also to personal power and self-esteem, as you think about the impact expectations can have.

**Expectations my parents had of me:**

to stay clean and tidy

to do well in all my exams

to look after my younger sister

always to be happy

to join the family business

to be honest

to get married young

to be instantly obedient

to keep my Mum company rather than going out with my friends

that I would work out what was right for me

**How I felt/feel about these:**

annoyed; too afraid to explore

under pressure to achieve

sometimes glad, sometimes resentful

frustrated and unheard

proud but trapped

a bit guilty at the time, now glad

angry and embarrassed

rebellious/intimidated/need to please

indignant/overburdened supported

**Unfair demands I may make on my child/children:**

to be tidy all the time

to share everything

never to be angry or rude

not to squabble or fight

not to be clumsy, noisy or forgetful

to be good/obedient all the time

never to take risks

**How they may be feeling:**

frustrated

unjustly treated

guilty, defiant

bewildered, misunderstood

inadequate

hopeless, ashamed

fearful, rebellious

## ☹ Unhelpful

## ☺ Helpful

## ☹ Unhelpful

## ☺ Helpful

# The Ways Children Develop

The journey through childhood, from being a helpless newborn baby to becoming an independent adult, is an extraordinary one. As parents, all the messy, noisy, energetic ways children explore and develop can seem more infuriating than miraculous. Let's look how children develop and learn new skills, and how we can help them by meeting their needs – physically, mentally and emotionally.

## Physical Skills

Includes learning to walk, skip, climb; co-ordination to catch a ball, ride a bike, drive a car; and fine muscle skills like tying shoelaces, threading a needle, using tools and a computer keyboard and icing cakes.

## Mental/Intellectual Skills

These develop as children learn to use their minds: to think, make sense of the world around them, talk and listen, read and write, have ideas and explore those of other people, identify problems and work out solutions.

## Social and emotional development

When children discover how to enjoy playing with others, to make friends, to sort out disagreements, to understand how they themselves feel, to care about how others feel.

There is such an emphasis on education in school, it's easy to forget that a huge amount of learning takes place in the first five years of life. Children are learning all the time. Don't be fooled by the idea that they're "only playing" – playing is the child's job!

### ❓ How can we best help our children explore and develop?

They need space to explore safely and to be active. They need toys and tools and equipment. These needn't be expensive, *e.g. for a young child:*

- saucepans and kitchen spoons make a great drum kit

- a roll of wallpaper lining lasts a long time when used as drawing paper

- garden canes and a sheet can be a den, a cave, a tent

- a bowl of washing up water and plastic mugs offer bubbles, pouring games, and the chance to get wonderfully wet

- a pile of cutlery is a good sorting game.

- Orange segments, apple quarters, biscuits or raisins can be counted, and as they are eaten even turned into a maths lesson

- if children are bored and restless, put on some loud music and dance with them until they're out of breath and ready to drop

- take them out to a park to run around, play hide and seek, fly a kite

**On the next few pages are charts to help you check how well your expectations of what a child can do match when they may actually learn.**

# Ages and Stages Quiz

**?** **Here's a selection of skills and attitudes children learn as they grow up. At what age do you think an average child might be able to do these?**

There are boxes for you to fill in on the next page, followed by completed charts on pages 168 and 169 for you to check your answers. Of course, there is really no such thing as an average child. Individual children are often ahead in some areas of development and less advanced in others. The quiz is intended to give a general idea of what we can expect as children develop and grow.

*appreciates another's point of view*

*begins to use words*

*can bath him/herself*

*can do simple ironing*

*can draw a person*

*can use child's scissors*

*catches a ball*

*chooses own friends*

*concentrates for up to 5 minutes*

*dry at night*

*enjoys baby talk*

*explores body parts*

*fears death*

*fears strangers*

*gets school things ready on his/her own*

*giggles about toilet talk*

*has 900-word vocabulary*

*helps care for pets*

*helps to put away toys*

*hops*

*identifies colours*

*lays/helps to clear table*

*learns to read/write*

*makes bed*

*makes choices*

*makes cup of tea/simple meals*

*manages pocket money*

*may adopt special comfort object*

*may be jealous of siblings*

*may have an imaginary friend*

*needs company, warm words and gentle touch*

*needs peace and quiet*

*needs privacy*

*not ready to share*

*plays sociably*

*prepares own lunchbox*

*puts toys away on his/her own*

*realises the impact of own behaviour on others*

*recognises the difference between deliberate and accidental hurt*

*responsible for doing homework*

*responsible for pets*

*rides a bike*

*smiles*

*sorts out minor squabbles*

*stays away with a friend*

*tells the time*

*understands "No"*

*understands jokes*

*understands that feelings affect behaviour*

*walks*

# Ages and Stages Quiz

**0 - 2 years**

**2 - 4 years**

**4 - 7 years**

**7 - 9 years**

**9 - 12 years**

# Ages and Stages Quiz - Examples

## 0 - 2 years

begins to use words

explores body parts (true of all ages)

fears strangers

may adopt special comfort object (also 4-7s, and even 7-9s)

may be jealous of siblings (true of all ages)

needs company, warm words and gentle touch (true of all ages)

needs peace and quiet (true of all ages)

not ready to share

smiles

understands "No"

walks

## 2 - 4 years

can use child's scissors

concentrates for up to 5 minutes

may be dry at night

enjoys baby talk

has 900-word vocabulary

helps to put away toys

identifies colours

makes simple choices

may have an imaginary friend

plays sociably from three years old

may still use special comfort object

## 4 - 7 years

can draw a person

catches a ball

chooses own friends

fears death

giggles about toilet talk

helps care for pets

hops

is dry at night

lays/helps to clear table

learns to read/write

rides a bike

understands jokes

understands that feelings affect behaviour

may still use special comfort object

# Ages and Stages Quiz - Examples

## 7 - 9 years

appreciates another's point of view

can bathe him/herself

makes bed

prepares own lunchbox

puts toys away on his/her own

tells the time

realises the impact of own behaviour on others

recognises the difference between deliberate and accidental hurt

sorts out minor squabbles

stays away with a friend

may still use special comfort object

## 9 - 12 years

can do simple ironing

gets school things ready on his or her own

makes cup of tea/simple meals

manages pocket money

needs privacy

responsible for doing homework

responsible for pets

To help our children develop in every way – physically, mentally and intellectually, and socially and emotionally – sometimes it's best to follow rather than lead them. If we offer them different activities they will soon let us know which ones they enjoy.

We can also discover what sort of play is right for a young child by watching what other children do, by looking at the suggested age range on toys in shops, by going to the family centre, nursery, etc. for advice and for the child to try new activities.

As children get older, they have clearer ideas about what they want to do, and are more able to tell us. They are also, of course, increasingly influenced by their friends and by what they see on television.

Children need more than toys. They need our time – to keep them company, to tell them stories (reading them or making them up), and to help them without doing a takeover bid for their play. Children have a great need to play; it's how they learn. They are explorers, scientists and artists. If we offer them activities that are right for their age and stage of development, we will meet their needs and, by containing the mess, meet our needs too. If they have to do it all for themselves, we're likely to get upset with the results.

| If you... | ...they are less likely to... |
|---|---|
| let a child play at the sink, pouring water from a jug into plastic mugs and back again | pour milk all over the table |
| make pens and plenty of paper available, and display the results | scribble on your newly decorated walls |
| give a corner of the garden, a packet of seeds of their own, and a bit of help | damage your precious plants |
| have fun running around the park | run riot at home |
| let them help you cook | be fussy about their food |
| encourage them to talk, and really listen to them | whinge for your attention (and more likely to listen to you, too) |

All the way through their childhood and adolescence, children need us to give them new experiences that are right for their age. They also need us to take an interest in what they are interested in, as well as introducing them to what we enjoy. Chores take longer with a toddler helping, but you're teaching useful skills to a willing learner, and they won't do much harm with a duster or a rubber hammer! We have only ourselves to blame if we push away a four-year-old keen to join in, and later find ourselves with a clumsy teenager refusing to help around the house.

If we can enjoy our children's learning while they are young, we'll help them want to go on exploring and learning new things all their lives.

# Helping Children Grow Up

**The goal in raising children is to help prepare them for life as adults.**

When we are wondering how to respond as parents, it can be helpful to think about the qualities we admire in people we know, and to ask ourselves how we can help our children gain these qualities too. For example, we may admire people who are reliable and do what they have agreed to do, people who are considerate towards others and also know their own minds, people who can look after themselves in practical ways, people who cope well with life's stresses and strains.

The need to help our children become competent and feel capable is obvious, but we may lose sight of it in the daily rush, or be so used to doing everything for babies that we forget to step gradually back, and give background support as they get older. Our job is to help them learn what they need to know so they can run their own lives by the time they are grown up. This doesn't happen by magic on their 18th birthday – it's a long process.

When they are very young, we need to exercise control over children to keep them safe; as they grow, we need to empower them, encouraging them to take on new tasks and responsibilities that will make them confident and independent. This is not always easy. We need to allow children to make mistakes, to be forgetful or careless or lazy, and also (as long as they're not in danger) to experience the consequences.

My children are eleven and fourteen, and they expect me to do everything for them, however much I nag at them. What else can I do?

"You can stop waiting on them. If we don't want to be treated like doormats, we have to get up off the floor! Starting with things that matter to them, explain that you've decided it's time for a change, that you're happy to show them what they need to do but won't go on doing it for them. In the time you save by doing less and nagging less, have some fun!"

# Different Types of Parent

Let's think about parents who control and parents who empower. Do you recognise yourself in any of these descriptions, either what you do as a parent or what happened to you when you were a child?

## ☹ Parents who control

*Here, let me make the sandwiches for you. I'll make you egg ones today.*

**Parent behaviour**

Does everything for children; over-protective.

**Effect on child**

Child becomes lazy and demanding, feels helpless and incapable.

## ☺ Parents who empower

*What have you decided to put in your sandwiches today?*

**Parent behaviour**

Helps child to acquire practical skills and to be responsible.

**Effect on child**

Child becomes and feels capable, gains in confidence and uses initiative.

## ☹ Parents who control

*You should practise more. Then you might get chosen for the team like John did.*

**Parent behaviour**

Often criticises and nags child, makes constant comparisons between siblings.

**Effect on child**

Child becomes resentful and frustrated, sibling rivalry increases.

## ☺ Parents who empower

*You're doing really well – you're so quick around the pitch you get past almost everyone!*

**Parent behaviour**

Focuses on what the child does well, has a positive attitude to their efforts.

**Effect on child**

Child gains in confidence and self-esteem, is willing to try new activities.

## 😞 Parents who control

*You only got a B in your maths mock? You should have been able to get an A.*

**Parent behaviour**

Constantly urges children to do better – nothing is ever good enough.

**Effect on child**

Child becomes discouraged and may stop trying, or may become over-anxious about achievement and turn into a perfectionist.

## 🙂 Parents who empower

*You got a B in your maths mock? Well done – I know you find it hard.*

**Parent behaviour**

Has reasonable expectations of children, enjoys and encourages their successes, offers positive, non-critical advice – sometimes!

**Effect on child**

Child takes pride and pleasure in activities, learns to be realistic about own abilities; self-esteem not dependent on constant success.

## 😠 Parents who control

*Why did you break that? I bet you did it on purpose. You're not to be trusted!*

**Parent behaviour**

Does not trust children: is suspicious.

**Effect on child**

Child learns not to trust others, feels guilty, may become deceitful.

## 😃 Parents who empower

*Your toy's broken? Let's see if we can mend it.*

**Parent behaviour**

Trusts child and is trustworthy; when child owns up is not angry.

**Effect on child**

Child learns to tell the truth, takes responsibility, trusts others.

## ☹ Parents who control

> *Behave yourself. What will people think of you being such a cry-baby?*

**Parent behaviour**

Needs children to be cheerful and well-behaved at all times – demanding, or anxious about being judged by others.

**Effect on child**

Child learns to suppress emotions, may become sullen or a people-pleaser, or may become aggressive and rebellious.

## ☺ Parents who empower

> *Injections hurt, it's fine to cry. Come and have a hug.*

**Parent behaviour**

Is sensitive to child's feelings; clear boundaries while accepting that children take time to learn how to behave.

**Effect on child**

Child learns that it is all right to have different feelings and moods – and learns to respect those of other people.

## ☹ Parents who control

> *Give me the list. I haven't got time for you to decide what you want to take on the trip.*

**Parent behaviour**

Must dominate and "win" in all situations – is always right.

**Effect on child**

Child becomes argumentative or gives up trying to think for him/herself.

## ☺ Parents who empower

> *You find the things you think you'll need, and then we'll go through the list together.*

**Parent behaviour**

Helps child to work things out; respects child's opinions.

**Effect on child**

Child becomes confident, learns to make decisions and use own initiative.

# Growing Up Checklist

As our children grow, there are several traps we can fall into. We may become over-controlling; we may expect the children to do more than they are yet able to do; we may go on doing things that the children are quite capable of doing for themselves, and turn into a doormat or a martyr! It isn't always easy to know when we're getting it right for ourselves and our families, but if there's a lot of resentment around the chances are that something is wrong.

One way to check out how well we are helping our children learn to become capable and independent is to talk through this list with them, and find out what they are ready to learn. If necessary, show them what to do – and then let them do it! It isn't only the skill they gain – they also learn to take responsibility for the task. Only step in if their failure to do something is harmful, such as a pet suffering because it hasn't been fed. If you agree with a teenager that he's responsible for his own washing, and he discovers at the last minute that his favourite shirt isn't clean for a party, that's his problem, not yours.

- Making the bed
- Tidying bedroom
- Choosing clothes
- Dressing
- Tying shoelaces
- Tidying up toys
- Getting up in time
- Making school lunches
- Getting breakfast
- Making tea, toast
- Cooking, washing up
- Washing face, brushing teeth
- Having a bath on your own
- Laying and clearing the table
- Helping with housework
- Putting away clothes
- Sorting out disagreements
- Feeding/caring for pets
- Ironing

- Crossing road without holding hands
- Crossing road alone
- Doing homework unsupervised
- Going to the local shop
- Making phone calls
- Making appointments (doctor, etc.)
- Choosing TV programmes/DVDs
- Cleaning the car
- Navigating on journeys
- Organising time for homework/fun
- Painting and decorating
- Gardening
- Mending bicycle punctures
- Deciding how to spend pocket money
- Earning money
- Arranging when to see friends
- Choosing/buying presents
- Travelling without an adult
- Having a boyfriend/girlfriend

# coping with stress

**Life can be stressful – that's hardly a new idea! The fact that it's as true for children and teenagers as it is for us may not be so obvious.**

When life is tough, it can be hard to recognise the signs of stress in ourselves. It's all too easy to feel overwhelmed, powerless, angry with other people, etc. rather than face up to the fact that we're feeling stressed and need to do something about it. We handle difficult situations more easily if we are looking after ourselves well: if we're feeling very stressed, it's a sure sign that we need to nurture ourselves more.

Children and teenagers often can't tell us in words when they are feeling stressed, but they will show it in the way they behave. It is helpful if we can recognise their signs of stress, rather than labelling them as "naughty" or "lazy".

It isn't always possible to prevent stressful situations, for a child or for ourselves. Even so, there are ways of making these difficult events easier to cope with. We can be sensitive to the signs of stress in ourselves and in others. We can find what helps to relieve our stress, and what works for them. We will feel better and cope better ourselves, and if we help our children find ways to reduce their stress, we'll be giving them an important skill for life.

On the page opposite we've listed some of the many situations that can be stressful for children. You will probably be able to think of some more. We have included some ideas for how children may feel and how they may behave when they are stressed.

**Take some time to think about how people in your family react to stress, and whether any difficult behaviour can be traced to uncomfortable feelings resulting from stressful events.**

Here's another Nurturing Programme slogan:

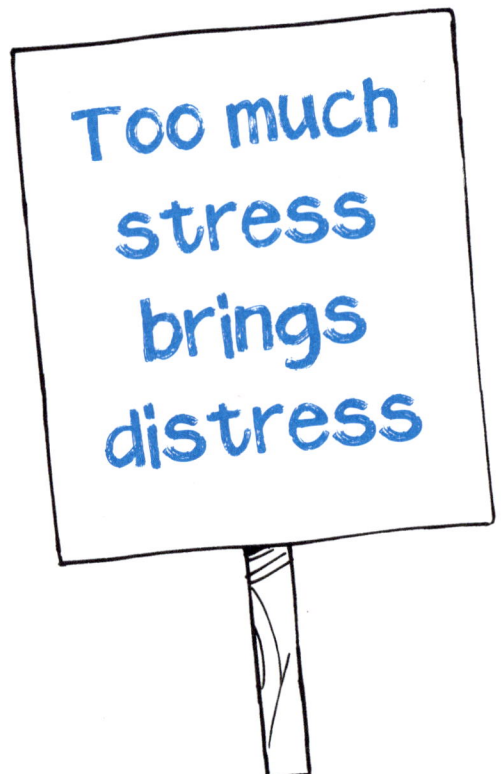

Too much stress brings distress

# Situations children/teenagers find stressful:

parents' absence/restrictions/threats/attitudes

favouritism

hostile neighbours

birth of brother or sister

parents' stress

starting or changing school

being bullied

falling out with friends

lack of privacy/space

learning difficulties

being unpopular

being nagged

moving house

illness

too-high expectations

death of pets

SATS and exams

competitiveness

rejection

false accusations

not having what other children have

labelling

criticism

forced relationships

parents' separation/divorce

journeys

long punishment

parents' depression/anxiety/anger

parent's new partner

death in the family

car accidents

erratic routines

hostile teacher

feeling afraid/inadequate

physical, verbal, sexual abuse

inconsistent discipline

loneliness

witnessing violence

Christmas/birthdays/holidays

## How children/teenagers may feel:

| | | | |
|---|---|---|---|
| confused | overwhelmed | unwanted | inadequate |
| anxious | unloved | jealous | lonely |
| angry | depressed | insecure | bad |
| sad/miserable | frightened | resentful | guilty |

## How children/teenagers may behave:

| | | | |
|---|---|---|---|
| clingy | pick on others | take foolish risks | withdrawn |
| defiant | wetting/soiling | truancy | stealing |
| cry a lot | tantrums | poor concentration | lying |
| swearing | lack initiative | | fighting |
| destroy things | obsessive | sullen | arguing |

When we're caught up with feeling stressed it can be incredibly hard to believe that anything could make a difference. Thinking this is a sure sign of a stress emergency! We tend to believe that the problems are entirely beyond our control, that there's nothing we can do. As a result, when we're feeling stressed we usually also feel angry, overwhelmed, depressed, upset, trapped or helpless – just as the children and teenagers do. You may recognise these feelings from the Power Quiz in Session 4 (see page 93): they go with feeling powerless.

But we aren't completely powerless, even though it can feel that way. We always have our personal power, which we looked at in detail in Session 4. Taking good care of ourselves when life is difficult is a very positive way to use our personal power.

It's easier to think of the things that help us when we're stressed at a time when we're not, when life is going more easily. We need to find ways of staying calm, or at least of calming down, ways that help us to relax, that help us hold on to a sense of perspective, things we enjoy that can lift us out of our misery. It's also good to know who we can reach out to for support when we need it – relatives, friends or professionals. There are no right and wrong answers. All that matters is to know what works for you. It could be:

| going for a swim | having a hug and a cry | baking cakes |
| digging the garden | sawing logs | talking to a friend |
| lying in a hot bath | listening to music | |

And if this list is starting to sound familiar, it's because many of the ways we recover from angry feelings, and ways we nurture ourselves, stand us in good stead when we get stressed, as well as helping us keep out of the stress danger zone.

If you know what works for you and make a note of it, in an emergency you can turn to your list and choose something. Even though at the time there may be a stressed, impatient voice in your head saying "It won't work! I can't! There's no time! Leave me alone!", the fact that you yourself wrote down these ideas means you may feel more able to try one of them.

**On the page opposite there's space for you to record what helps you keep stress at bay. It's a good idea to talk with the family about what helps them, too. A child could make a poster as a colourful reminder of what helps them to "chill out" when times are tough.**

# our Family's Stress Busters

What works for me...

.............................................................................

.............................................................................

.............................................................................

.............................................................................

.............................................................................

What works for my child/children...

.............................................................................

.............................................................................

.............................................................................

.............................................................................

.............................................................................

# The Effects of Labelling

When we are children, we are often given labels. Adults (not only parents!) may describe us again and again as if a particular way we behave is Who We Are. Usually these are unhelpful labels, such as *"She's so fussy"*, *"You're naughty"*, *"He's stupid"*, *"You're such a nuisance"*, *"You're so selfish"*, *"She's always obstinate"*. Sometimes people apply helpful labels. These include: *"She's such a sweet little thing"*, *"You're wonderful"*, *"He's no trouble at all"*. Or they may be double-edged, as in: *"You always have an answer to everything"*.

It's the repetition that turns an observation into a label. We hear the same words over and over again, until they come to define us.

I am a bad person.

I'm so excited, but I can't show it.

There's no point in trying.

So I'm nothing but trouble – I'll show them!

LITTLE DEVIL

QUIET

USE-LESS

HERE COMES TROUBLE

If we think about labels, it becomes clear that all of them are limiting. Because we have to believe what adults tell us about the world when we're young, we believe what they tell us about ourselves, too. We usually live up or down to people's expectations, and fulfil their judgements of us. We often carry our labels into adult life; it takes great strength to dare to be different.

## Here are some things to think about:

- adults may react differently to the same behaviour in different children.

- adults tend to give unhelpful labels to children whose personalities are different from their own, e.g. an energetic "doer" may label a quieter child "lazy" or "dreamy," while  dult may label a lively, sociable child "over-excited" or "too boisterous."

  els describe children critically for qualities that are admired in adults, e.g.  'e" becomes "interested", "stubborn" becomes "determined."

  ls depend on gender, e.g. a man may be labelled "soft" and a woman "gentle."

w Up

Think of the labels that were put on you when you were a child, and how you felt about them. If you'd like to, write down the labels and the feelings. It can help then to cross out the labels – they are someone else's out-of-date opinion, not who you really are.

Label .......................................................................

Feeling .......................................................................

Label .......................................................................

Feeling .......................................................................

Label .......................................................................

Feeling .......................................................................

When you're ready, try to think of any labels you may be putting on your child or each of your children, and write the child's name and the labelling words or phrases if you'd like to. With older children, you could ask their opinion, too, and talk with them about it.

Labels on

Labels on

Labels on

Labels on

**? How do you think the child might feel about the labels he or she is carrying?**

It can be quite painful to remember the restricting or hurtful labels we were given, and thinking about what we might be inflicting on our children can be painful too. Take a break if you need one.

# The Art of Listening

One of the greatest gifts we can give each other is to listen. Being listened to really well, attentively and kindly, encourages trust, honesty and openness between people. It's a great way to improve communication in all our relationships, and particularly in how we relate to our children.

It sounds so easy, and yet it isn't always that easy to do...

**?** **If someone is talking to you, how often do you find yourself being distracted by your own thoughts?**

**?** **Or interrupting to give good advice or talk about something similar that happened to you?**

**?** **Or getting on with doing a chore so they have to follow you around?**

**?** **Or having a running commentary in your head along the lines of "What a fuss about nothing!", "I wouldn't have done it like that" or "No wonder you got into trouble".**

Even if we don't say anything, we signal our reactions to what the other person is saying, sending subtle messages by the expression on our faces and our body language – our gestures, the way we sit, and so on.

If we can switch off to ourselves, and really switch on to the other person, focusing on what they are saying, and tuning in to the feelings behind their words (that's empathy at its best), it makes a world of difference.

Here are some helpful and less helpful ways of listening.

**☹ Unhelpful**

**☺ Helpful**

If someone finds it hard to talk, we can sometimes make it easier for them by doing something together that still allows us to listen with all our attention, and at the same time make the focus a bit less intense.

**In our busy lives, how often do we stop, and do nothing other than listen closely to what someone else is saying?** This can be hard to do with other adults, and for some reason even harder with children. And yet it's so important. If we encourage our children by listening to their happy chatter, they will feel more able to talk to us when they have a problem. And they may even choose to go on communicating with us when they become teenagers – a group who sometimes come in for more than their fair share of being talked at rather than listened to!

**Have you been using bedtime Praise Power, which we suggested in Session 5?**

A great addition to this is to get into the habit of listening to whatever the child wants to say, without interrupting, correcting, advising or doing anything other than simply listen. We can do this at other times of day too, of course. It just feels extra-special at bedtime.

# REFLECTIONS

HOW do I peel off the labels my parents put on me? It feels odd to think that I could believe what I think I'm like now, and not be stuck with what they said I was like all those years ago.

I'm going to think a lot more about what I expect of my two. I demand a lot of my son, and I think I treat my daughter as though she's still practically a baby.

My parents always urged me to do my best, but my best was never good enough! I think I go to the other extreme, and don't really encourage my child to try at anything.

I'm always telling my children to listen to me. Perhaps I should listen to them more as well.

Thinking about how much there is for children to learn, and how important we are in helping them learn all they need, can feel a bit overwhelming. But nature is clever, and has programmed children to find out what they need to, when they need to. All we have to do is give them lots of opportunities, and stay aware of what they seem to need. Their needs change all the time, so we can be sure they'll keep us on our toes!

You might like to think back to the very beginning of the Programme, when we invited you to think about your hopes and goals as a parent. One aim many parents have is to help their children be the most that they can be, to find their own place in the world. If we are sensitive to a child's developmental needs, this is just what we will be helping them to do.

# REFLECTIONS

**?** **What are you thinking and feeling at the end of the seventh session? If you would like to, record your own ideas here.**

........................................................................

........................................................................

........................................................................

........................................................................

# Time to Have a Go

Discuss the growing up checklist with children, and ask them when they think is the right time to take on any of the tasks. Include your teenagers.

Go on using Nurturing Programme approaches such as Choices and Consequences to help children feel capable. Keep up the bedtime Praise Power – and practise listening extra well.

Give yourself a treat.

# Session 8: Keeping children safe

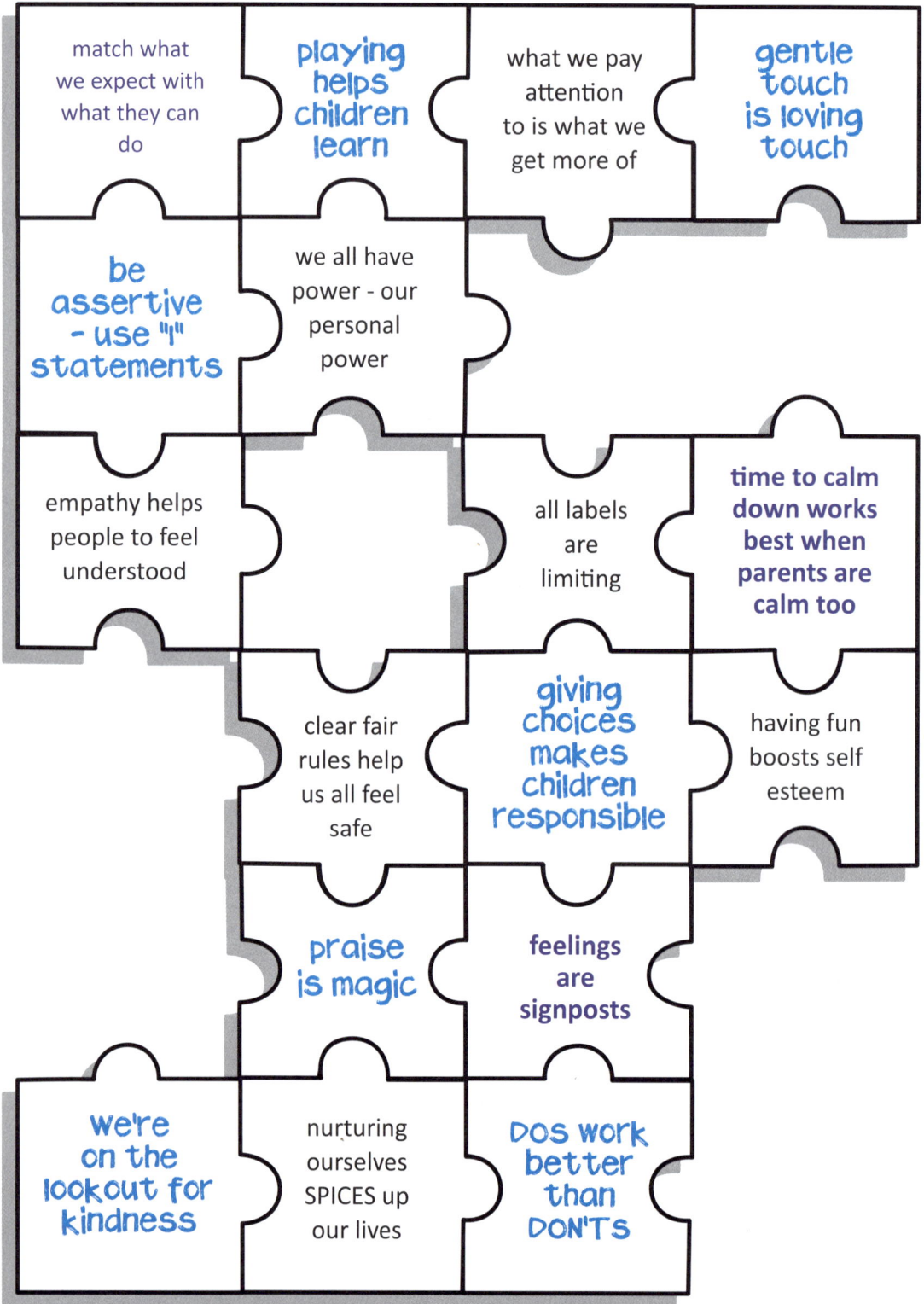

match what we expect with what they can do

playing helps children learn

what we pay attention to is what we get more of

gentle touch is loving touch

be assertive - use "I" statements

we all have power - our personal power

empathy helps people to feel understood

all labels are limiting

time to calm down works best when parents are calm too

clear fair rules help us all feel safe

giving choices makes children responsible

having fun boosts self esteem

praise is magic

feelings are signposts

we're on the lookout for kindness

nurturing ourselves SPICES up our lives

DOS work better than DON'TS

# Feedback: What Parents Tell Us

### Growing up checklist

"My son didn't want to go through the list, until he realised he could choose what he wanted to try. Now he's proving how capable he is, he's proud of himself."

### Praise Power

"Having a happy time together at the end of the day has helped the children settle down and go to sleep quickly."

### Nurturing Programme approaches

"When things get tough I still lose it, but at least I can think afterwards about what went wrong and what I could try another time."

### Nurturing Programme approaches

"I'm finding it easier to stay calm and think about how to react. Choices and Consequences helps me not to fly off the handle so much."

**?** **What have you tried so far, and how is it going? Make a note of how you're getting on if you'd like to.**

### Growing up checklist

"My daughters got really competitive, so I talked to them separately about it."

I had a go at...

and the result was...

# Keeping children Safe

**It's a strange fact that we are surrounded by images to do with sex, and yet it can still be a difficult subject to talk about. In this section, we'll be looking at issues around sex and relationships, particularly focussing on keeping children safe both in the real world and in the digital world.**

For many of us, there's a hangover from the past, when sex and sexuality were taboo subjects. If we feel uncomfortable or negative about our bodies, or have painful memories in relation to sex, it is even harder to have a relaxed and open attitude when it comes to helping our children understand about sex.

When we talk about sexual issues with parents, we find that everyone wants to help their children develop a healthy attitude. We also find that many of us think our own parents' approach wasn't very helpful.

**If we are not comfortable ourselves talking about sex, it's likely to make it more difficult to have open and helpful conversations about it.**

It is also helpful to talk about sex in the context of relationships. From an early age, it is important for children to have some sense that sex is about people and how they connect and interact with each other. If we lose sight of this, the whole issue might start to seem a purely mechanical or functional process. Parents are often relieved to discover that it isn't a question of having to say it all at once, and get it right.

Children are naturally curious about their bodies, and helping them learn about how bodies work is a process that starts when they are very young. If we can deal with sex-related topics as they arise, a child is more likely to grow up feeling comfortable about them. If we keep sexual issues quite separate, and say nothing until they are reaching puberty, we make life more difficult for them and for ourselves.

Don't we talk to children too early about sex? Isn't it better to wait until they ask us questions before we say anything?

**"You're right. It is helpful to respond to children's questions in an age-appropriate way. However, children are sensitive to our attitudes, and may be afraid to ask us about something we never mention."**

The media bombard young people with sex as though it's the only thing that matters. How can we get them to think about sex responsibly – and to take care of themselves?

"Everything we do, all through their childhood, to encourage respectful, warm, empathic relationships, and to build their self-esteem, will stand our children in good stead when they start to explore sexual relationships too."

There are some very good books to read with a child (see page 251) that can help us deal with topics we aren't sure about.

Perhaps the most useful thing of all is for us to take a look at our own attitudes to sex and sexuality, and to think about what messages we want to pass on to our children that will help them become confident and responsible in their own sexual lives.

## How we learn about sex

Humans come in all shapes and sizes, but not all shapes and sizes are valued equally in all cultures. We often judge our own body harshly because we fall short of a stereotype of what is attractive. Yet if we think of our friends, we realise that we choose them because we like them as people, not for their looks. If we grew up being taught that bodies were shameful, were criticised for the way we looked, or overheard adults judging people by their appearance, we may be ill at ease in our own skin.

**You might like to think about how you feel about your body, and what you would change about it if you could. Ask yourself why you'd like to be different – and whose standards you're trying to live up to!**

If we accept our own body, and like ourselves despite its imperfections (just as we do our friends), we give positive messages to our children. If we value our body and look after it well, we will encourage our children to do the same. It's a good first step in helping them feel comfortable about sex as they grow up.

**?** How did you find out about sex when you were young?

**?** Did adults tell you what you needed to know?

**?** Did you get information from friends, magazines, TV, the Internet, sex education at school?

**?** Did what you learnt, and the way you found out, help you to feel confident and comfortable?

**?** Were you embarrassed or ashamed?

**?** What makes it easy for children to ask questions, and what makes it difficult?

Many people remember their parents' awkwardness, and want to be more natural with their own children. Some were told almost nothing, and were anxious when a wet dream or a first period took them by surprise. Some regret being told simply the mechanics of sex; some resent the moral agenda that was forced on them; some asked a simple question and were given a long explanation that went over their heads. But others report having families who were open and relaxed, and who helped them to think of sex as both normal and special.

Here are a couple of examples of Unhelpful and Helpful ways of talking to your children when they ask questions:

As we shall explore later, children may also gain knowledge and information about sex and relationships via the digital world.

# Graffiti Wall

Let's look at some of the words people use to describe sexual parts of the body and sexual activities.

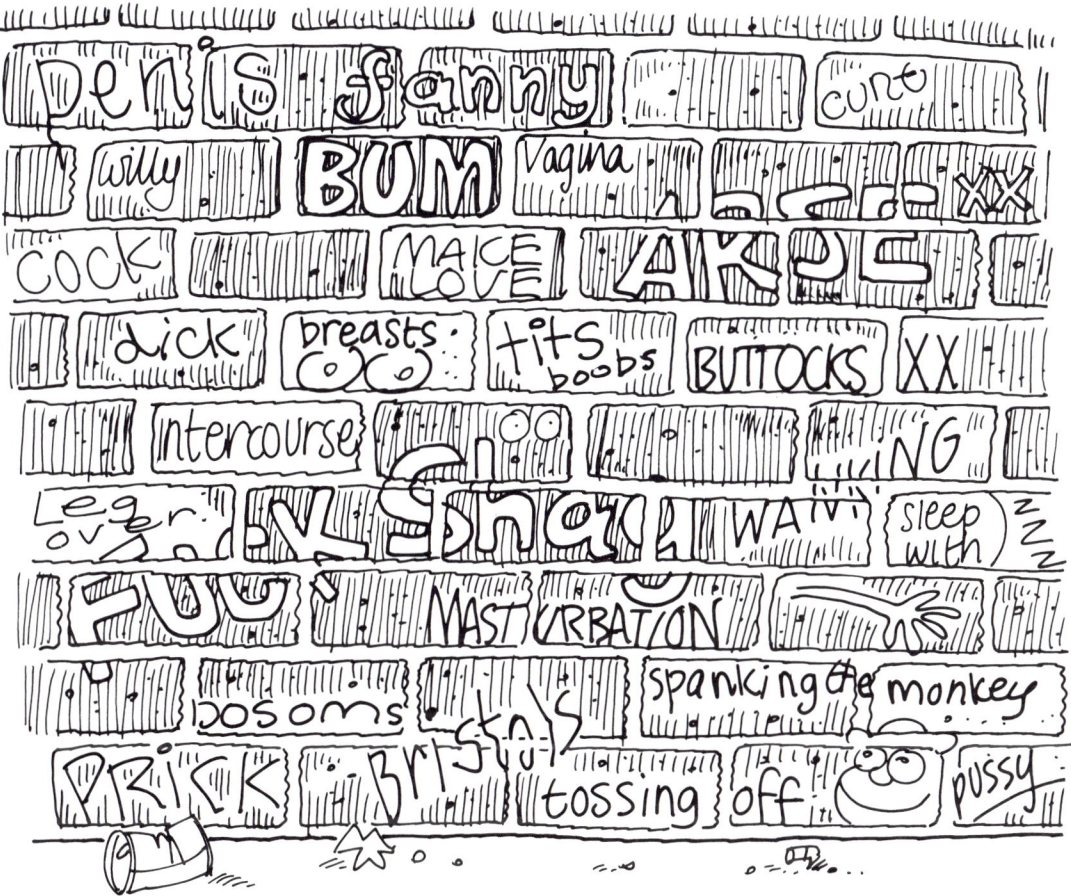

❓ **Why are there so many more slang words for sexual parts than there are for other parts of our bodies – a knee, toe or elbow, for example?**

Many of the words are used as insults or have aggressive overtones, so they send very mixed messages.

❓ **What does it suggest to talk about body parts and people in this way?**

Whether or not we use these words, approve of them or find them offensive, our children will hear them. One of the reasons for talking with our children about sex is to offer a gentler, more respectful and loving context than the one they hear about on the street and in the media.

# Developing a Healthy Attitude to Sexuality

## What helps

feeling secure and loved

affectionate adult relationships

open communication in the family

trust and acceptance

answering questions honestly

healthy self-esteem

seeing warm adult relationships

being physically affectionate

well-presented relationships and sex education at school

respecting the child's body throughout childhood

encouraging the child to respect/value their own body

helping the child use their personal power in a positive way

## What gets in the way

unhealthy self-esteem

lectures on wrongness of sex

parental shame/discomfort with body

over-emphasis on the importance of looks, body size, etc.

controlling child's friendships

child's need for affection not being met

poor family communication

lack of trust, resentment

misleading information from peer group

pressure from peer group

some messages from TV/DVDs/ internet/gaming

hostile adult relationships

# Questions children Ask

This isn't a complete list, as children will always surprise us. It's good to be sure we have an answer to the questions that are bound to come up, and sometimes to have ways of providing answers even before the questions have been asked.

How are babies made?

what's an orgasm?

what are wet dreams?

why do girls have periods?

why don't girls have a willy?

How do babies get out?

If sex is for making babies, does that mean you and Dad have only had sex twice?

why do grown-ups have hairy bodies?

what does 'wanking' mean?

what if I come across something horrible on the internet?

what is an erection?

Is it normal for one breast to be bigger than the other?

can you use a tampon if you're a virgin?

what if someone asks me to send a picture of myself?

*If you find you can't answer these questions, you need to discover more before your children put you on the spot!*

# Questions Parents Ask

There are no cut-and-dried answers to these questions, though we have given some suggestions here. It's good to think about them, and perhaps to discuss them with other parents, seek advice from books and magazines, or ask a health professional or teacher.

Is it a good thing or a bad thing for children to see adults in the nude?

"If everyone is comfortable and it is genuinely natural, then it's fine. As they get older, children usually prefer more privacy for themselves and from you – and this should be respected."

Is it a good idea to tell boys as well as girls about periods, and girls as well as boys about erections, wet dreams, etc?

"Yes, it's helpful if both understand what happens to female and male bodies."

What should I do if I find my child masturbating?

"It's normal for young children to 'play with themselves'. As they get older, children need to be told that it's OK, and is something to do in private. A child who constantly masturbates needs help."

When should you tell a child about sex?

"From 3 to 18 years old, as opportunities come up and whether or not they ask. You don't have to do it all in one go!"

# Helping Children Stay Safe

**We are all concerned about keeping our children safe from harm.**

One particular anxiety is in relation to sexual abuse. While children are – rightly – taught about "stranger danger", most sexual abuse is inflicted by someone the child knows. More girls than boys are abused, but it does happen to boys too.

The issues are much broader than simply focusing on the need for children to be alerted to possible danger. Many of the topics we have already looked at in previous sessions are relevant. Building children's self-esteem, encouraging them to use their personal power, helping them to think for themselves by giving them choices, treating them with respect, giving them the affection and approval they need – all these help children to trust their own judgement, to become resilient and to look after themselves in many different and difficult situations. The less vulnerable children are generally, the less likely they are to be a target for abuse.

One way we can help to protect our children is to teach them to heed their feelings of discomfort around touch. Any touch that gives a child an "ugh-ugh" feeling is, to them, inappropriate touch. If we make a child kiss someone when they don't want to – an uncle with a tickly moustache or a friend of ours they hardly know – or sit on someone's knee when they would rather not, we teach them to suppress their instincts about touch. In an unsafe situation they will be more vulnerable, as they will have learnt that they have no right to object to touch that they do not like. So the best way we can protect our children is to make sure we treat their bodies with respect; then they will expect others to do so too.

As a man, with so much media focus on sexual abuse I've become anxious about whether it's all right to cuddle my daughter or bath her. Are you saying I shouldn't?

"No, definitely not. Affectionate touch from both parents meets boys' and girls' need for physical closeness and helps them learn the difference between touch that feels OK and touch that doesn't. As they get older, we should just be sensitive to their need for privacy."

# Gender Stereotypes

There are many different ways in which children and young people learn about relationships. It might be helpful to consider the different ways we might limit children's opportunities or treat them differently because of their gender.

choice of toys

books

TV/films

friends

language used

games/sports

expectations, e.g. future jobs/careers

attitudes expressed and modelled

Expected behaviour

Of course, some of this we may be completely unaware of – or it might be that we are acting in the same way as, or the opposite way to, our own parents. It's worth thinking about the potential consequences of this. If we are able to allow children a wide range of opportunities, it is likely that we'll be helping them to -

- Have access to many more games, toys, books, etc.
- Be open-minded about other people
- Develop healthy attitudes and relationships
- Be themselves
- Broader opportunities for jobs/careers
- Lead fuller and happier lives

To enable children and young people to thrive, it helps to offer a wide variety of opportunities and to enable them to be themselves.

# Respecting Children's Space

We can show our respect of our children's bodies and their "personal space" in many different ways throughout their childhood. Here are some examples.

☹ **Unhelpful**

☺ **Helpful**

☹ **Unhelpful**

☺ **Helpful**

☹ **Unhelpful**

☺ **Helpful**

# Keeping Private Parts Private

We can help protect our children by teaching them that parts of their body where it is easy to cross their hands/arms are private, and should not be touched by anyone except to keep them clean or if they are ill and need to be examined by a doctor. Nor should anyone ask the child to touch them in these places.

In Session 6 we thought about kinds of touch: nurturing touch, hurting touch, and scary touch. Any touch that is either physically or emotionally uncomfortable can be scary. One more reason for not using any kind of hurting touch in the way we discipline our children is the message it sends – that it is all right for other people to do things to your body that you do not like if they are older, stronger or more powerful than you. If we use only welcome, gentle, nurturing touch with our children, they will grow up with the best protection against inappropriate touch.

# Family Attitudes

Children learn from the environment and culture in which they grow up. It can be helpful to consider your own family attitudes and cultures relating to our bodies.

Reflect on attitudes in your family to: *nudity, bathtime (sharing & privacy), privacy in bedrooms* and to think about what lies behind these views and behaviours.

- **?** **Are you comfortable with these, and are your children comfortable? Would you like to change anything?**
- **?** **How much is linked with our own childhood experiences?**
- **?** **What are the implications of all the different stances on these?**
- **?** **Are there links with body image?**

*What is important to remember* is that there is no one correct way and that it is helpful to think through these issues - being clear about what is important to you as a family and that everybody in the family feels comfortable with how things are.

# Keeping Safe in The Digital World

We've spent time looking at what might influence children in the "real" world. It's important also to consider this in the context of the digital world.

We know that the digital world, in all its versions, is an integral part of children's and young people's lives. Children now access the online world at an early age. This is very different from previous generations. For most young people, the use of social media is one of the key ways in which communication with friends, family and the outside world happens. It is clear that the digital world has transformed the way in which children and young people relate to each other.

While different elements of the digital world impact on children and young people at different stages, it is all part of a wider picture. In addition, parents generally feel more equipped and confident having thought through the issues before they are immediately faced with them.

While there are huge benefits to these digital opportunities, there are also risks. The expert view tends to be that it is often counter-productive to rely on filters and restrictions. The key message is that communication and talking is the most helpful approach. This can help children to develop their own thinking about this topic and is a great way of letting children know that parents care and are interested in their well-being.

It is helpful for parents to be clear about the messages they would like to be giving children on this topic and important to equip young people with the knowledge and information necessary to manage their digital and online activity safely.

Just as in the "real" world, it is important that children respond appropriately if they experience "ugh-ugh" feelings in the digital world. Some of the ways in which children might feel unsafe or even be getting into trouble in the digital world could include:

- Seeing inappropriate images

- Developing unhealthy relationships with other people

- Feeling out of their depth

- Making a mistake by saying or seeing something they regret or feel uncomfortable with

# Tips for Keeping Children Safe in The Digital World

✓ Encourage discussion about digital activity

✓ Be open

✓ Emphasise the importance of talking with you, especially if they feel unsafe

✓ Let them know you're there to listen, especially if they have made a mistake or regret doing something

✓ Make use of helpful information on websites such as those below

✓ Try to be non-judgmental

✓ Be clear about boundaries and expectations

✓ Talk about healthy relationships

✓ Discuss the risks

Many children and young people spend a large amount of time using a variety of digital devices. It is helpful for parents to think about what boundaries to set around this. There is a great deal of evidence highlighting the fact that the blue light from digital devices has a negative impact on children's sleep. For this reason, it is helpful to have a clear boundary around devices at bedtime – for example, no devices in the last hour before bedtime.

For many parents, this may be a very difficult subject to tackle but it is also extremely important – remember that talking about it is key. Knowing that key adults are there for them will help children to navigate this tricky area, enable them to feel supported and safe if and when things don't go to plan and to feel more confident and equipped to develop healthy relationships.

**There are many useful websites available for parents, such as:**

**nspcc.org.uk** (National Society for the Prevention of Cruelty to Children)

**ceop.police.uk** (Child Exploitation & Online Protection Centre)

**ceopeducation.co.uk** (National Crime Agency's CEOP Education)

# Time to Relax

This session is a difficult one for some parents, so here is another relaxation exercise. As before, you can read it for yourself, pausing to tense and relax the muscles in turn, or ask someone to read it to you, or record it.

We'll relax by finding tension in our bodies, and letting go of it.

Take your attention to your feet... curl your toes as tightly as you can...

and now let them uncurl and relax.

Next clench the calf muscles at the back of your legs...

hold them tight... and let go and relax.

Now tighten your thigh muscles, as strongly as possible...

hold it... and let go and relax.

Now tense your tummy muscles... and let go and relax.

Now clench your hands into a fist... and let go and relax.

Now hunch up your shoulders... and drop them down and relax.

Now tense the muscles in your face... and let them relax again.

To check your breathing, put one hand high up on your chest,

and the other on your tummy.

Notice which hand moves as you breathe in and as you breathe out. Begin to take longer, slower breaths so your lower hand moves and the upper hand stays almost still. Breathe in slowly and easily... breathe out slowly and easily... breathe in... breathe out... and with every breath, let the breath get longer, and softer, and lower, and easier...

Breathe gently in this way for a while, until you feel calm and relaxed.

And remember, whenever you want to pause or be calm, you can put a hand on your tummy to remind you, and let your breathing soften and slow down.

# REFLECTIONS

I remember my parents turning off the TV if anyone had so much as a sexy kiss. No wonder I find it really embarrassing to talk about sex! I don't want my children to feel so awkward.

We often tell children to do as they're told, but we need to give them the right to say no about some things and to stop when other people say no, like siblings tickling each other too much.

I'd never thought about how to be specific when warning my children about unwelcome touch.

It hurts to remember what went on when I was a child. If only my Mum had told me that nobody was allowed to touch my private places, perhaps I'd have been able to tell somebody what was happening.

There's a lot of food for thought in this session, and not only about explaining the mechanics of sex to children. It's a chance to think about the unspoken messages we give about how we feel about our bodies, about respecting our children's bodies and their right to their personal space, about touch and intimacy. It links to all the ways we are helping them grow into confident, resilient people who will respect other people and themselves.

Anyone who has been sexually abused, or has a child who has been sexually abused, may have a strong emotional reaction to this session. If it seems overwhelming, it may be a good idea to talk to someone close to you or to seek professional help. The long-term effects of sexual abuse can be devastating – that's why we think it is so important to include this topic in the course.

# REFLECTIONS

**?** **What are you thinking and feeling at the end of the eighth session?**
**If you would like to, record your own ideas here.**

........................................................................................

........................................................................................

........................................................................................

........................................................................................

# Time to Have a Go

SUN   MON   TUES   WED   THURS   FRI   SAT   SUN   MON   TUES   WED   THURS   FRI   SAT

Think about whether you are having honest and open discussions with your children around sex and relationships - and what would help.

Have a look at information on the recommended websites.

Try to check in with your child about their internet/social media use.

Play an extra game with your child or children, go for a coffee with your teenager.

Think of free/cheap family games you or others you know enjoy.

# Session 9:
## Behaviour to Ignore, Problem Solving and Negotiating

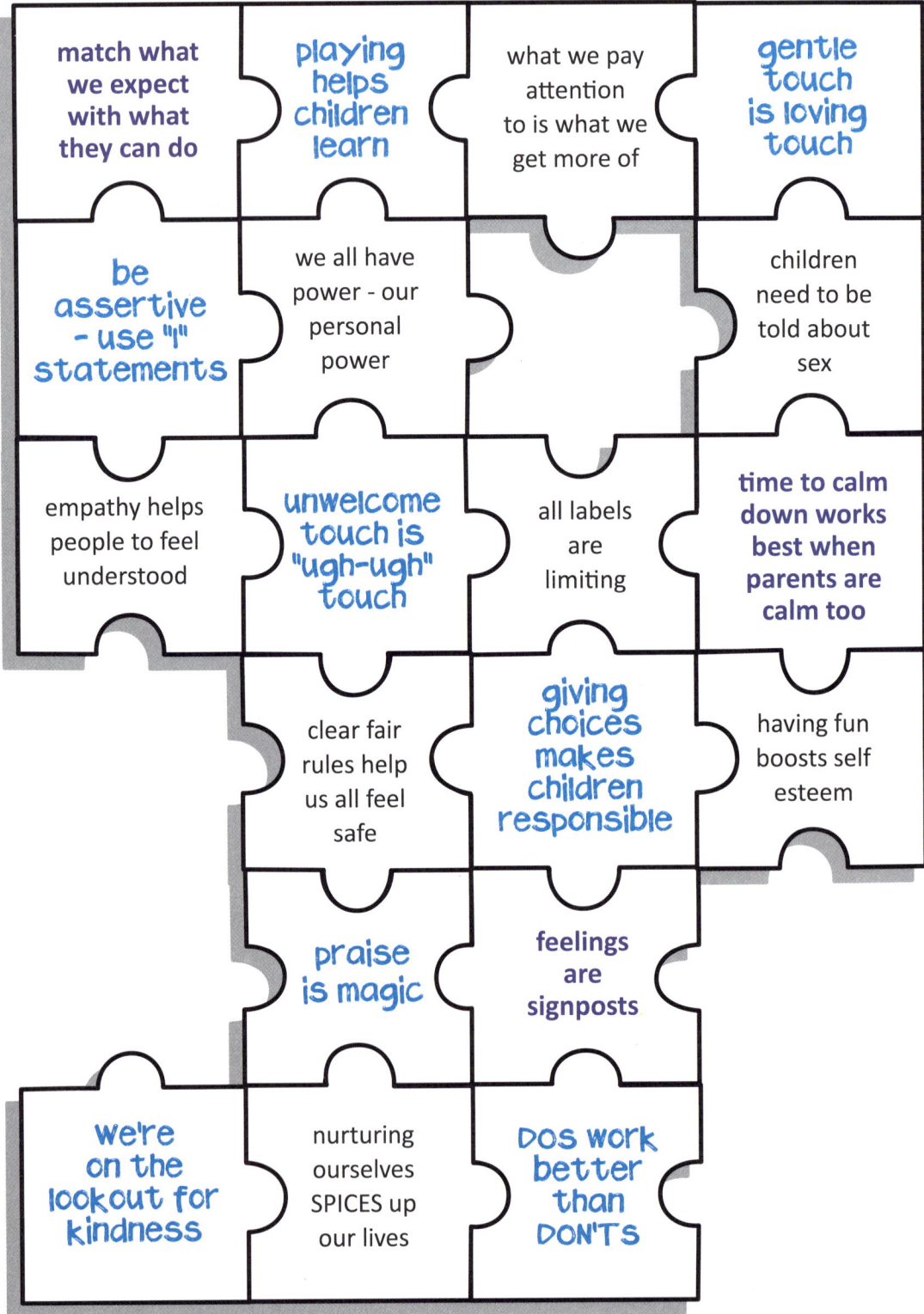

match what we expect with what they can do

playing helps children learn

what we pay attention to is what we get more of

gentle touch is loving touch

be assertive - use "I" statements

we all have power - our personal power

children need to be told about sex

empathy helps people to feel understood

unwelcome touch is "ugh-ugh" touch

all labels are limiting

time to calm down works best when parents are calm too

clear fair rules help us all feel safe

giving choices makes children responsible

having fun boosts self esteem

praise is magic

feelings are signposts

we're on the lookout for kindness

nurturing ourselves SPICES up our lives

DOS work better than DON'TS

# Feedback: What Parents Tell Us

## Messages about sex and sexuality

"I'd always thought it would be better to wait until the children are older before telling them about sex. Now I can see it may be easier and better to help them find out bit by bit so it's part of everything they're learning rather than being separate."

## Give yourself a treat

"When I get the chance to recharge my batteries, I find it so much easier to be patient with the family."

## Family Games

See parents' ideas in Time to Play on page 210.

## Messages about sex

"We read Mummy Laid An Egg together and had a good laugh. I think it's shown that I don't mind them asking me questions."

**?** **What have you tried so far, and how is it going?**
**Make a note of how you're getting on if you'd like to.**

I had a go at...

and the result was...

# Time to Play

You probably have some favourite family games. Here are some ideas for cheap or free games, some for the family to play together and others to entertain young children while you get on with what you need to do (once you have helped them set up the game if they are too young to organise it themselves). It's also worth remembering that chores for adults can be fun for children: even a feather duster can turn into a toy, and when the child is bored of housework they can use their imagination to turn it into something else (a witch's broomstick, perhaps?).

*garden obstacle course/ jumping course*

*space rocket/ship to sail the high seas (get a cardboard box from an electrical store)*

*cooking together*

*home disco dancing*

*memory games*

*giant jigsaw (keep out on table, board or tray)*

*telling ghost stories (great by candlelight)*

*giant picture (use wallpaper lining)*

*board games and card games*

*hide and seek*

*dressing up*

*kitchen picnic (under table with blanket to make a den)*

*children's puppet show/play/concert*

*grow a garden wigwam (bamboo poles and runner beans)*

*treasure hunt*

# Behaviour to Ignore

**We often say to children, "Just take no notice – you'll only make it worse", when they are annoyed by their brother or sister. Yet many of us find it hard to take our own advice when it comes to taking no notice of the trivial, annoying ways children may behave.**

It's tempting to correct children every time their irritating minor habits or fidgeting grate on our nerves. But nagging about these minor ways of behaving seldom works, and it can sour the atmosphere between us and the child. There is another way.

We have left the idea that some behaviour is best ignored until now because it is perhaps one of the hardest methods to use. It only works if we can develop the self-control not to react, and to divert our attention away from the behaviour we don't like. But like toothache, once we have noticed something we find annoying, it's quite a challenge to think about anything else!

It can also be hard to believe that something will stop if we pay no attention to it. This may seem strange, but it's often true. When we were thinking about family rules, rewards and penalties in Session 3, we noticed that behaviour that attracts our attention tends to be repeated. This explains why it can be so effective to ignore some behaviour.

Children need our attention, and will try to get it in any way they can. If we pay attention to the behaviour we do want, the behaviour we don't want sometimes just goes away. Likewise if we can respond to the feelings behind the behaviour, the difficult behaviour itself often stops. We can't and shouldn't take no notice of potentially dangerous or harmful behaviour – that needs to be dealt with in one of the ways we have explored in earlier sessions.

I'd give anything for the pointless bickering to stop. Are you saying that if I ignore the kids when they're having a go at each other they'll stop doing it?

"There's an important difference between ignoring what they are doing and ignoring them altogether. Bickering is often about the children needing our attention; we need to respond, and yet make sure that we give attention for something other than the behaviour that we find annoying."

**?** Are any of these ways of behaving and our reactions to the behaviour familiar to you? What others are true for you?

## what not to ignore

behaviour that risks harm to people or property;

a child's distress

fighting, hitting, etc.

crying because hungry, hurt or frightened

tantrums (recognise their frustration; don't give in; comfort when storm over)

wetting or soiling

obsessional/ phobic behaviour

crying because afraid of the dark, monsters, nightmares

head banging

spitting

running off

being a nuisance in public

deliberate damage

angry offensive language

## what we might ignore

whining/ whinging/using baby talk

hair-twiddling

fiddling with Velcro on shoes

thumb-sucking

interrupting

nose-picking

swearing

showing off

nagging

stammering (wait patiently)

demanding things in shops

calling out from bedroom (after pleasant bedtime routine is finished)

crying for attention (when plenty of positive attention is already given)

low-grade rudeness/sullen looks

...........................................................

...........................................................

...........................................................

## How we feel/react

get really irritated

anxious about what other people will think

OK when I'm calm

take myself off

lights a fuse when I'm stressed

answer back in a whiny voice

want to scream

can bear it for a time, then snap at them

nag at him till he stops or goes away

get sarcastic

...........................................................

...........................................................

...........................................................

# Steps for Active Ignoring

**1** Be sure about what you want the child to do that would replace the unwanted behaviour

**2** Ignore the behaviour for as long as it lasts unless it gets dangerous

**3** Do not mention the behaviour directly (e.g. by telling the child you are going to ignore what they are doing, or by asking the child to stop) or indirectly (e.g. by mimicking or criticising)

**4** As soon as the unwanted behaviour stops, praise the child - not for stopping what they were doing, but for starting to do what you like (and look out for other opportunities to praise the behaviour you like, too)

**5** Ignore the behaviour, not the child as a person. If the behaviour gets worse, it is probably because the child is being ignored altogether, rather than being paid (positive) attention for something other than the unwanted behaviour

**6** Think about asking others in the family (e.g. partner, older children) to ignore the behaviour, but without any ganging up or siding with one child against another

**7** Think about the reasons behind the behaviour, and what feelings in the child may be triggering it (e.g. upset, frustrated, hungry); if possible address the problem without drawing attention to the behaviour that has made you aware of it

**8** Ask yourself what feelings this annoying behaviour may trigger in yourself, and how you could deal with/recover from/let go of them

what
we pay
attention
to is what
we get
more of

Children sometimes do things we find annoying to attract our attention. If we give them positive attention when they're behaving well, and ignore the unwanted behaviour while staying positive with the child, their behaviour often improves. Here are some unhelpful and helpful ways of responding to unwanted behaviour.

Unhelpful

*Why do you two always start arguing the minute my back's turned?*

Helpful

*It's so nice when you share your toys and have fun together.*

Unhelpful

*whinge whinge whinge*

*Shut up! I've got to make the shopping list, and I can't think straight with you whinging at me all the time.*

Helpful

*whinge whinge whinge*

*Let's make a shopping list. Will you write it for me while I check what we need?*

Unhelpful

*Don't go, don't go. My tummy hurts!*

*Stop making such a fuss – you know I've got to catch the train.*

Helpful

*Don't go, don't go. My tummy hurts!*

*Let's have a cuddle before I go – I'll miss you too.*

# Problem Solving and Negotiating

**As our children grow up, they need to learn how to make decisions, how to solve problems, and how to negotiate.**

It doesn't matter whether they grow up to be a long-distance lorry driver, a scientist, an athlete or stay at home to bring up a family – whatever life we lead, these are useful skills. They stand us in good stead too, of course, in sorting out difficulties and disagreements in the family and with friends, work situations, and so on.

Learning and using these skills lowers tension and reduces head-on conflicts. What often happens is that when two people have different ideas on something, there's a stalemate. Both people want to win the argument, and become deaf to the other person's point of view. The ways we respond to challenge, which we thought about in Session 5, come in again here: if we can be assertive and respectful, and if the other person can do this too, we're more likely to solve the problem. The hard part is to think clearly – never an easy thing to do when we're in the grip of strong emotions.

So we're going to look at ways of working out solutions to trying situations. Having a clear set of steps to follow can help to keep us thinking clearly, and focusing on finding a solution rather than blaming someone else for creating the problem in the first place. We'll think first about problem solving – what to do when there's a problem and you're not sure what to do about it, and then about negotiating – what to do when there is disagreement about the problem and/or the solution.

When I'm worried or upset about something I find it really difficult to think clearly my thoughts just go round and round in circles. Are you saying this can help me think through the situation?

"That's the idea. When our thoughts and feelings get tangled up it can be so hard to look for solutions. Having clear steps to follow is a way of focusing our attention on what we can do to deal with the situation."

When we take steps to solve a problem we may be clear about what to do. If someone else is involved in the problem, we may need to negotiate before arriving at a decision.

Here's a situation that we use in groups to show how problem solving works. Most parents can identify with the problem of getting everybody ready in time for school and work – the morning routine can be stressful and chaotic.

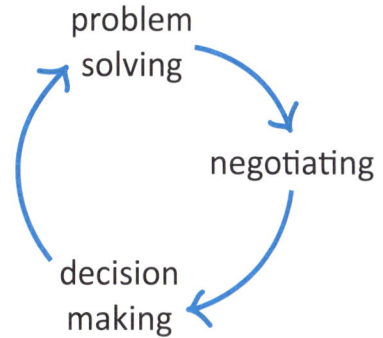

On the next page the steps for problem-solving are listed in more detail. You might like to check them against this family's discussion.

# Steps for Problem Solving

**1** Work out exactly what the problem is. If it is complex, you may need to break it down so you are only trying to solve one problem at a time

**2** Be clear about whose problem it is. Sometimes what may be a problem for you is not a problem for someone else (e.g. teenagers' messy bedrooms may suit them fine!)

**3** If others are involved, discuss what has already been tried to deal with the problem. Presumably these efforts were not successful, or the problem would not still exist; try to avoid blame and fault-finding

**4** Consider/agree what the goal is - what would solve the problem? This is the crucial step: identifying what would be a solution. Make the goal reasonable and achievable (with children, make it appropriate for their age, too)

**5** Think of as many ways as possible to reach the goal. Welcome all ideas at this stage; let children come up with crazy as well as sensible ones

**6** Decide which solutions to try. Pick one or two workable ideas from the list of solutions, and have a go

**7** If the problem remains, go back to the list, check step 1 and step 4 again, and try some other ideas. If none of them works, you may need to try negotiating instead

Before working out a problem with the family, you might like to have a go at thinking through a problem using the practice sheet to guide you.

Choose something manageable to begin with – not the most difficult thing you've ever had to confront!

# Practice Sheet
## Problem Solving

What exactly is the problem? ....................................................

........................................................................................

........................................................................................

Whose problem is it? .............................................................

........................................................................................

What has already been tried? ................................................

........................................................................................

What is the goal - what would solve the problem? ...................

........................................................................................

Ways to reach the goal: ........................................................

........................................................................................

........................................................................................

What to try: ..........................................................................

........................................................................................

........................................................................................

# Steps for Negotiating

1. Work out that there is a difference of opinion

2. Invite the other person to give their point of view

3. Reflect the other person's view back to make sure you have really understood it

4. Give your point of view

5. Ask the other person to reflect back your point of view, to make sure they have understood it

6. Offer a compromise that takes both views into account

7. If your compromise isn't acceptable, invite the other person to suggest one

8. Continue to negotiate until a compromise is agreed

Here's an example of successful negotiation. It doesn't always go quite as smoothly as this, of course – learning to negotiate takes time, like any other new skill!

# The Nurturing Toolbox

There's an old saying: If you only have a hammer, everything looks like a nail. As we come to the end of The Nurturing Programme course, let's see what tools there are in our Nurturing Toolbox. These give us a whole range of things to try in the many different situations we come across in the family.

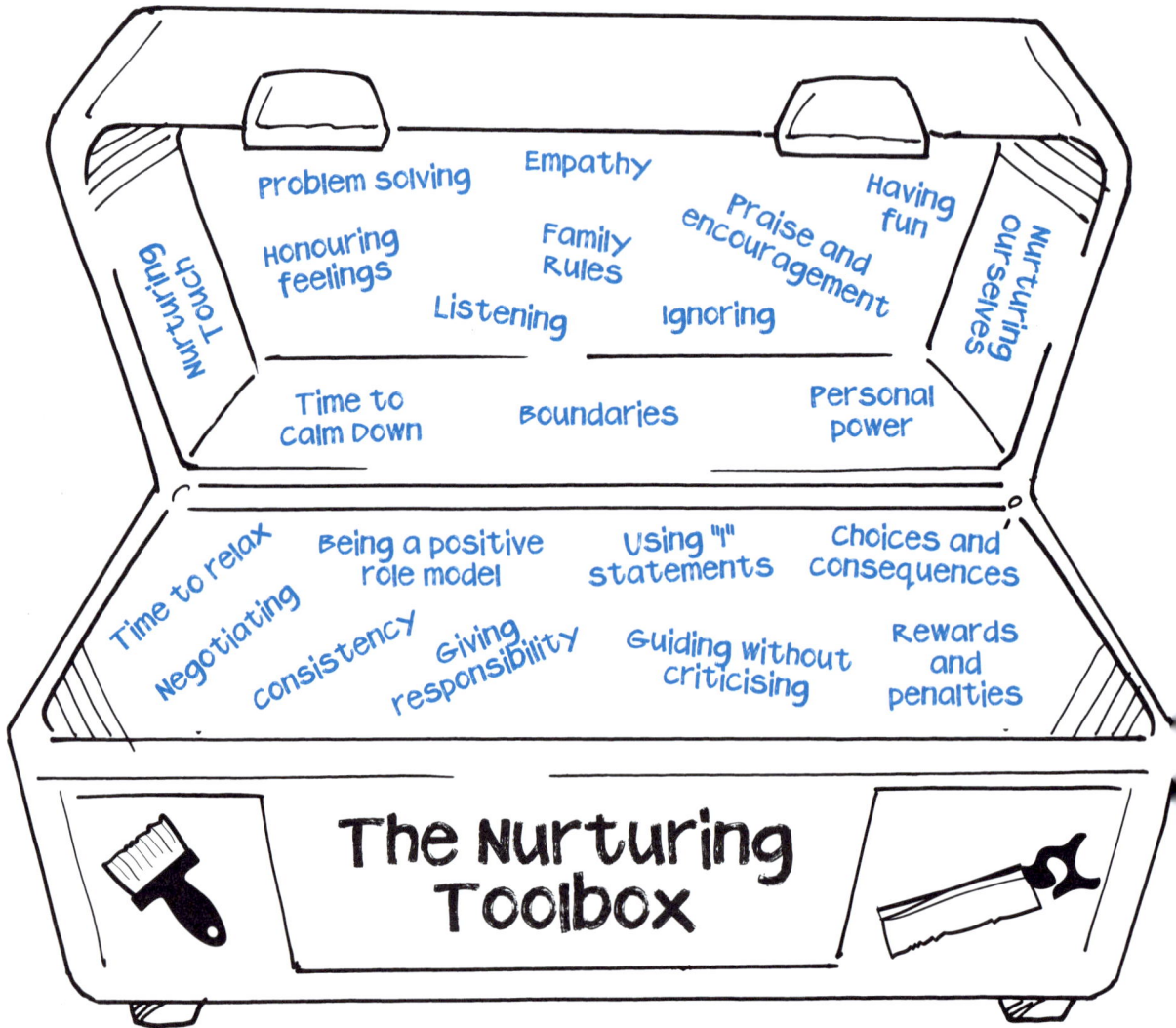

Problem solving

Empathy

Having fun

Praise and encouragement

Honouring feelings

Family Rules

Nurturing Touch

Nurturing ourselves

Listening

Ignoring

Time to Calm Down

Boundaries

Personal power

Time to relax

Being a positive role model

Using "I" statements

Choices and consequences

Negotiating

Consistency

Giving responsibility

Guiding without criticising

Rewards and penalties

**The Nurturing Toolbox**

These are all useful approaches, particularly when used alongside positive emotional investment in the family – see Session 10.

**Here's a way of revisiting the ideas and approaches we have explored. As you go through the list, notice how far you have come, what still needs more time and effort – and what you might like to think about some more!**

One positive thing I said to a child this week was ........................................

An example of when to use Time to Calm Down is ........................................

One of our family rules is ........................................

One thing I reward my children for is ........................................

I like to use my personal power by ........................................

One way of helping a child's self-esteem is to ........................................

My child feels good about him/herself when I ........................................

Choices and Consequences that work well in our family are ........................................

When a child feels jealous of a brother or sister it might help to ........................................

If a child is very critical of others, s/he might be feeling ........................................

If a child shouts a lot it might help to ........................................

One way I help my children feel happy at bedtime is ........................................

One way I calm myself down when I'm angry is ........................................

An "I" statement I made recently was ........................................

Instead of using hurting touch or wounding words, I can ........................................

One way I nurture myself is ........................................

Gentle, nurturing touch I like to give/receive includes ........................................

One responsibility my child enjoys is ........................................

Responding comfortably to questions about sex helps children ........................................

A behaviour I could ignore in my child is ........................................

An issue in my family that problem-solving might help is ........................................

Instead of arguing when we disagree, we could ........................................

When I really listen to a child's point of view, I find that ........................................

Something I am more relaxed about than I used to be is ........................................

One thing I like about my family is ........................................

*Please remember to congratulate yourself on things that are going well, and to be realistic in your expectations of yourself and your family.*

# REFLECTIONS

Those steps for solving problems seem a bit formal, but maybe it's good to start off like that while we get used to the idea.

Nobody ever told me about how to work out problems or negotiate. My parents were always right, and that was that; we just did as we were told. No wonder I find it hard to make decisions!

We've been having a stressful time at home recently; I don't think much has changed. I've still got the ideas and notes, so I can have a go again.

I've suddenly understood why things sometimes get worse rather than better when I nag at the kids over the little things.

This is quite a practical session, and it also links new ideas to things we've thought about before. Thinking about behaviour we could ignore brings us back to praise and a positive attitude; problem-solving and negotiating are part of clear and respectful communication. Hopefully the puzzle pieces are beginning to fit together in your minds!

That's what the review of ideas is about as well: showing how everything links up to make family life easier and more fun for everyone. Some families find at this stage that the Programme supports much of what they were already doing; others find it helps bring about a big change; for others, it takes longer for change to happen. Someone once said that the longest journey begins with the first step – that's true of nurturing parenting, too.

# REFLECTIONS

........................................................................................

........................................................................................

........................................................................................

........................................................................................

# Time to Have a Go

SUN   MON   TUES   WED   THURS   FRI   SAT   SUN   MON   TUES   WED   THURS   FRI   SAT

Choose something to ignore - and practise ignoring it.

Solve a problem, make a decision, negotiate a compromise.

Put aside some extra time to have fun together as a family.

Complete the Family Log, preferably discussing it in the family first (see Session 10, page 230).

# Session 10: Continuing the Family Journey

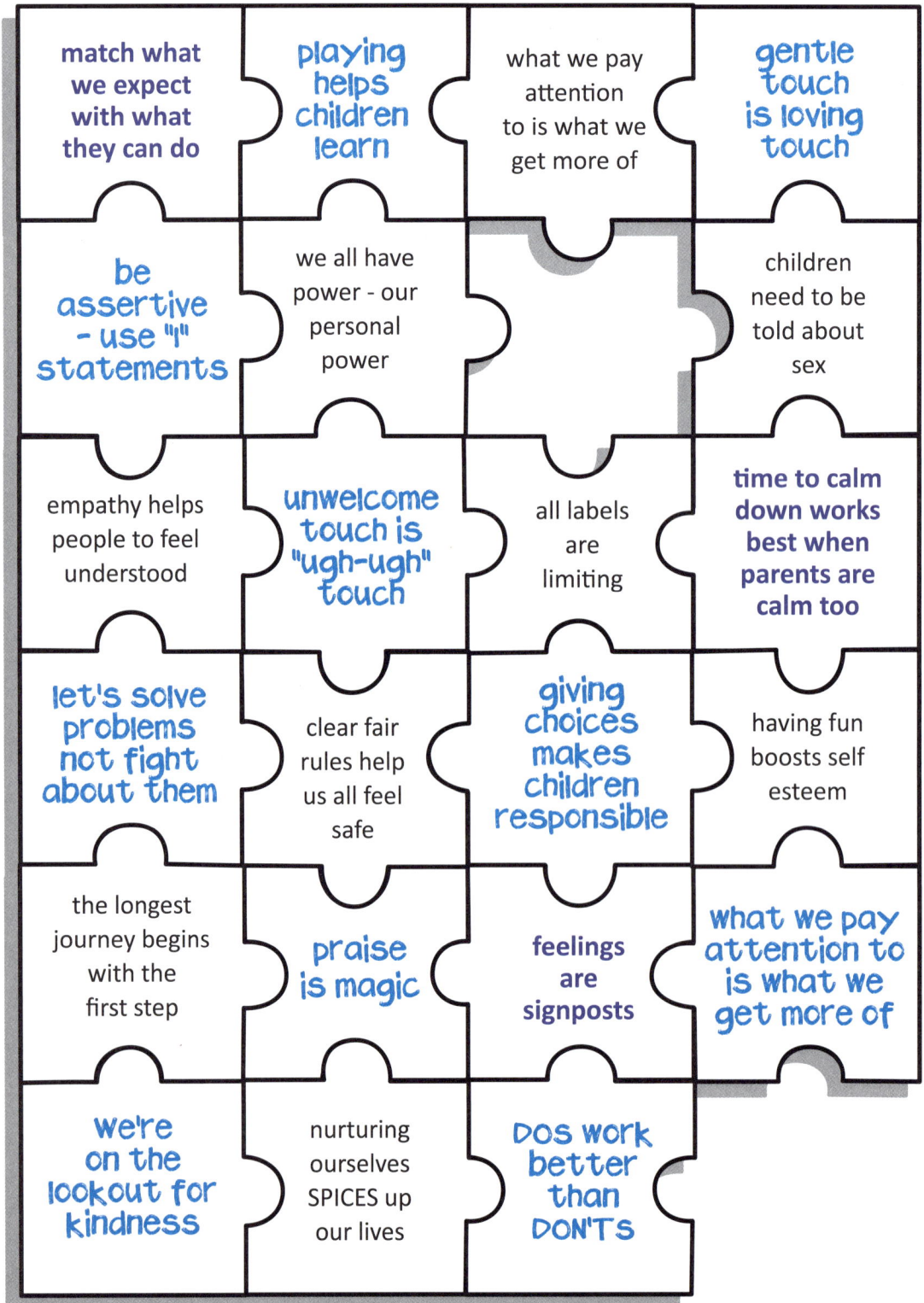

match what we expect with what they can do

playing helps children learn

what we pay attention to is what we get more of

gentle touch is loving touch

be assertive - use "I" statements

we all have power - our personal power

children need to be told about sex

empathy helps people to feel understood

unwelcome touch is "ugh-ugh" touch

all labels are limiting

time to calm down works best when parents are calm too

let's solve problems not fight about them

clear fair rules help us all feel safe

giving choices makes children responsible

having fun boosts self esteem

the longest journey begins with the first step

praise is magic

feelings are signposts

what we pay attention to is what we get more of

we're on the lookout for kindness

nurturing ourselves SPICES up our lives

DOS work better than DON'TS

# Feedback: What Parents Tell Us

### Family Log
"I think the person who's changed most is me. I'm much calmer and more able to think things through, and that seems to have a knock-on effect in the family."

### Ignoring
"It's so hard to ignore what they're doing without tuning them out altogether - I haven't cracked that yet."

### Problem solving and negotiating
"We talked about the getting-to-school-in-time morning chaos, and things are working much better already. Mealtimes are next on our problem-solving list!"

### Ignoring
"I'd never realised what a vicious circle I'd got into with my son. I'm really trying to notice when he needs attention, rather than just reacting when I feel annoyed."

**?** **What have you tried so far, and how is it going? Make a note of how you're getting on if you'd like to.**

### Having fun
"It's still hard to find the time, but I know we need to."

I had a go at...

and the result was...

# Taking Stock (Again)

At the end of Session 5 we invited you to think about what was happening in the family. At the end of Session 9, we suggested you do it again. Here is another chance to record your thoughts about the family's progress – and perhaps to compare them with the previous Family Log.

We have included a space for you to record what other members of the family think about how you are all getting on. Children are very perceptive, and often come up with shrewd observations!

## Family Log

How am I changing? ........................................................................................

.............................................................................................................

How do I think the family is changing? ...............................................................

.............................................................................................................

What do the family say is better? ......................................................................

.............................................................................................................

What ideas and strategies am I using confidently? ................................................

.............................................................................................................

Which ones would I like to feel more confident about? ..........................................

.............................................................................................................

What is the emotional temperature in the family?
*(Mark the thermometer for the whole family, and for individuals if you'd like to.)*

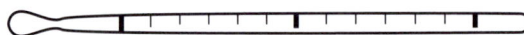

| cold | warm | hot |
|------|------|-----|
| critical | nurturing | angry |
| uptight | kind | shouting |
| contempt | respectful | critical |
| distant | fun | fighting |

# Where Have We Got To?

Here's another chance to reflect. At the start of Session 1 we invited you to think about where you were on the family journey.

❓ **How far have you travelled since then?**

You might like to think about how far you've come, and where you'd like to go. When you have thought about (and perhaps filled in) the two boxes you could compare them with what you thought and wrote at the beginning of the course.

How we are getting on as a family...

My aims/hopes/goals as a parent...

# Our Emotional Health

To lead satisfying lives and to be resilient in the face of life's difficulties, we need to be emotionally healthy. We mentioned some of the benefits of emotional health in session 1, and they can be represented by this diagram:

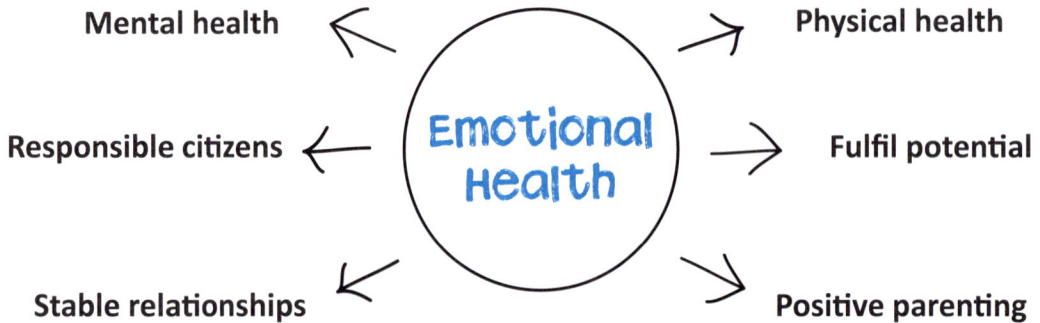

Mental health ← **Emotional Health** → Physical health

Responsible citizens ← **Emotional Health** → Fulfil potential

Stable relationships ← **Emotional Health** → Positive parenting

Some people refer to "emotional intelligence". We're all born with it; some people's childhood circumstances make it easier, and others' make it harder, for this intelligence to be developed so we become "emotionally literate".

**There are five main aspects of emotional intelligence we can develop:**

## Knowing our emotions

Self-awareness – recognising a feeling as it happens – is the first stage. We can eventually learn to stay aware, simply noticing the emotion rather than being overwhelmed by it, however turbulent we may be feeling at the time. This takes a lot of practice.

## Managing our emotions

Handling our feelings builds on our awareness of them. The aim is to be kindly in charge of our emotions rather than a helpless slave to them. It is helpful if we have ways of reassuring ourselves when we're feeling anxious, calming down when we're angry, soothing ourselves when we are sad. It is a question of balance: every feeling has its value and significance; it is the ratio of comfortable to painful emotions that determines our emotional well-being.

# Motivating ourselves

Harnessing our emotions to help us identify our goals and reach them – rather than letting emotions hamper our activities – helps us to achieve our aims. When we are distressed by difficult feelings, we can't "think straight"; when we are indifferent our motivation is low. When we are enthusiastic and confident, we are motivated and resilient, achieving more without getting stressed.

# Recognising emotions in others

Empathy, the ability to be sensitively aware of what another person is feeling, is the most important "people skill" of all, and a vital ingredient for satisfying relationships. It builds on self-awareness: the more open we are to our own feelings, the more skilled we become in reading other people's. We can sense how someone else is feeling by picking up subtle cues in their tone of voice, facial expression and body language – which together account for about 90% of how we communicate. People seldom express their emotional state clearly in words. When we want to be empathic it is best to be in an emotionally neutral state ourselves, or we may confuse our feelings with those of others.

# Handling relationships

Building on empathy, the art of relationships is based on skill in coping with emotions in others while also managing and expressing our own effectively. Emotions can be catching: whether we intend to or not, we transmit our moods and pick up those of others. Emotionally skilled people are great to be with. They are open and positive, and emotionally honest. We enjoy their rapport – the sense of connection between ourselves and another person. We can trust them with our feelings, and we feel good when we are with them. Learning these skills ourselves enhances all our relationships.

The Nurturing Programme helps to improve our emotional literacy and develop it in our children, so the whole family can enjoy the benefits of emotional health.

# Emotional Literacy Quiz

You might like to go through the quiz, pencilling a circle round one answer to each question, and come back to it in a few weeks' or months' or years' time to see what changes.

**1**   **Am I aware of my own moods?**

       not really      sometimes    often    yes

**2**   **Am I clear about what I am thinking?**

       not really      sometimes    often    yes

**3**   **Can I recognise what my body is telling me about my feelings?**
*(e.g. butterflies: I'm nervous; clenched fists: I'm angry; prickly eyes: I'm sad)*

       not really      sometimes    often    yes

**4**   **Do I acknowledge my powerful emotions comfortably?**

       not really      sometimes    often    yes

**5**   **Am I able to shift my mood?**

       not really      sometimes    often    yes

**6**   **Do I take my feelings into account when making a decision?**

       not really      sometimes    often    yes

**7**   **When I feel angry, do I erupt or become completely cut off?**

       not really      sometimes    often    yes

**8**   **Am I kind to myself when I feel anxious, sad, depressed?**

       not really      sometimes    often    yes

**9**   **Do I think of myself as determined?**

       not really      sometimes    often    yes

**10** Can I work today for tomorrow's rewards?

    not really    sometimes    often    yes

**11** Do I think of myself as optimistic?

    not really    sometimes    often    yes

**12** Can I respond positively to setbacks?

    not really    sometimes    often    yes

**13** Do I find it easy to admit when I am wrong?

    not really    sometimes    often    yes

**14** Am I comfortable telling others what I am feeling?

    not really    sometimes    often    yes

**15** Can I accurately sense what someone else is feeling from what they say, their tone of voice and body language?

    not really    sometimes    often    yes

**16** Do I usually make choices about how to behave that are helpful to me?

    not really    sometimes    often    yes

**17** Do I feel I have the power to be in charge of and for myself?

    not really    sometimes    often    yes

**18** Can I resolve the conflicts in my life satisfactorily?

    not really    sometimes    often    yes

**19** Do I think others really listen to me and try to understand things from my point of view?

    not really    sometimes    often    yes

**20** Do I really listen and try to understand things from others' point of view?

    not really    sometimes    often    yes

# Emotional Investment in the Family

In Session 9 we looked at the Nurturing Toolbox, which reminds us of all the different ways we can encourage co-operative behaviour in our children. Now we will think about the emotional side of family life, which is just as important.

Each of us has the equivalent of a personal emotional bank account; the family has a joint account. The more emotional investment there is in the family, the better off the family will be. We need to keep our own Nurturing Accounts topped up, as we can't give anything to our children's accounts if ours is empty. The same idea is recommended when we travel by plane: we're told that in an emergency, passengers with small children should fit their own oxygen masks before they put a mask on a child.

**?**   **Does looking after ourselves sound familiar?!**

*Here are some ideas for emotional investments:*

interests/skills/ideas · security · kindness · calm · admiration · empathy · fun · security · apologies · tolerance · openness · honesty · support · laughter · sharing · listening · hugs · encouragement · trust · praise · modelling-self · patience · caring · affection · friendship · loving · being positive · patience · problem-solving · respect · playing

**?** **Which of these feels important for your family? Fill in the coins with ideas from the list – and of course add any extra ones of your own.**

our family
nurturing account

If children are getting enough in their Nurturing Accounts overall, it won't matter if we don't manage to invest every day. The more we can invest, the sooner the children will be able to start "spending" the interest on the account's "funds" by themselves becoming nurturing towards other people. And on the inevitable bad days, everyone in the family – adults and children – will still have enough in their Nurturing Accounts not to go "into the red" and become emotionally overdrawn.

# continuing the Family Journey

So here we are – we've reached the end of the book. For parents attending a group, it's also the end of the course. We hope that you will feel better equipped to enjoy and cope with what happens on your family's journey now that you have The Nurturing Programme as your travel guide.

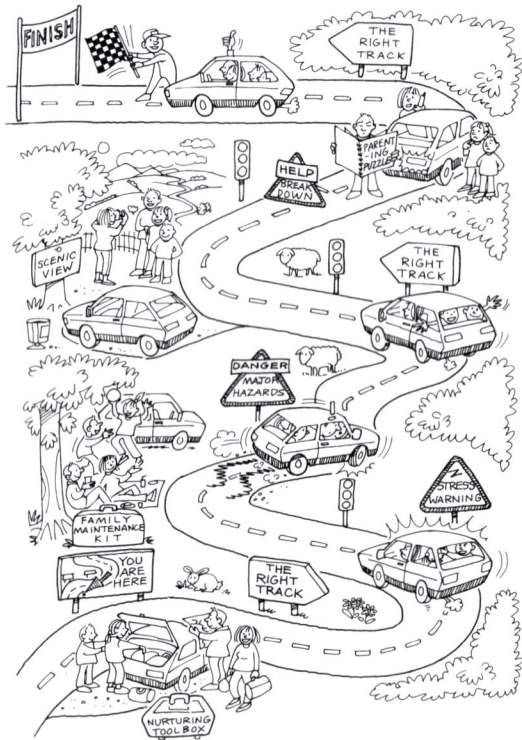

In one sense we've come to the end of a journey, the journey through the Programme. In another sense this is just the beginning – the start of the rest of your family's journey together.

On any journey we need to know where we're starting from and where we want to get to, to maintain the vehicle, to be alert to signs that we are on the right route or have lost our way, and to know what to do in an emergency. Sometimes it's fun to stop and explore; at other times getting lost can feel scary, and we need to go back to a familiar point and try again. On this page there's a map of the family journey, and on the next five pages we list some of the ideas that parents we have worked with in groups have had about it.

My older children are nearly teenagers. There's so much I wish I'd done differently. Have I left it too late to improve my relationship with them?

"I don't think it's ever too late. Being honest about what we regret, perhaps apologising to a child and listening as they tell us how they feel, making what changes we can now – all these can help to improve a difficult relationship."

As on other journeys, there will be times when you can stop and admire the view. When family life feels like an uphill struggle, it may be time to rest and get your breath back, to think about what else you could do to make the journey more of an adventure, or to recognise when you could benefit from some extra help (perhaps if there are too many hazards to cope with all at once, or if you're in an emergency situation). On page 244 there's space to note down what might help you to cope if times are tough – your emergency survival kit.

And remember – travel guides go with you, and can be referred to again and again whenever you want. Happy travelling!

# Emotional Traffic Lights

**(The feelings that fuel behaviour)**

**RED** — **feelings that may cause us to break down:** *fear, anxiety, feeling inadequate, anger, sadness, lack of skills, bitterness, confusion, criticism, humiliation, frustration, intimidation, shame, exhaustion, illness, past hurts*

**AMBER** — **feelings that may slow us down:** *uncertainty, worry, wobbly self-esteem, lack of motivation, embarrassment, fear of the unknown or of failure*

**GREEN** — **feelings that move us forward and help us get the best out of life:** *enthusiasm, vitality, praise, self-belief, curiosity, realistic expectations, confidence, feeling capable, sense of security, encouragement, rewards for effort as well as achievement, sense of fun*

# Where We Are Now

**(how far I've come and what we have learnt)**

more patience, humour, fun

more realistic

listening better – more sensitive

better teamwork

more empathy

better communication

more in charge

more self-nurturing

more confidence

less smacking/shouting

thinking about labels/comparisons

# Where We'd Like To Finish

**(long-term aims in our relationship with the children)**

to be friends so they trust/talk to us

understanding each other

to be happy

to love unconditionally

to respect each other's privacy

to cope with their rejection and keep our self-respect

to let go/not smother

mutual empathy

to "celebrate our differences"

accepting their partners into the family

# Tools We Have...

praise

choices and consequences

awarding responsibility

family rules

time to calm down

rewards and penalties

saying "No" and meaning it

"I" statements

setting a good example

ignoring annoying behaviour

honouring children's feelings

talking about how we feel

problem solving/negotiating

nurturing ourselves

# Tools We Have To Help Our Children

feel good about themselves

be positive and assertive

manage and communicate their feelings constructively

develop the skills to be resilient, thoughtful adults

develop the skills to be caring parents

make friends – and keep them

be honest

learn what we have learnt

be confident

value empathy and understanding

be accepting towards others

stand up for what they believe in

say "No" appropriately/stay safe

nurture themselves

# Family Maintenance Kit

## For parents

being listened to

time to myself, time with friends

managing anger constructively

being praised, praising myself

treats: flowers, listening to music, a peaceful bath, time to read

gentle touch: hugs, massage

time to relax

exercise: sport, going for walks

outings, breaks and holidays

positive thinking about myself

## For children

being listened to

being with friends

help with expressing my feelings

being praised, praising myself

sport and being able to let off steam

having fun with parents

gentle touch: hugs, massage

relaxing – doing my own thing

parents being interested in me

knowing parents are in charge

time to play

# Early warnings (Signs of stress)

### in adults

impatience

exhaustion

depression

anger

shouting

hitting

not sleeping

tearful

uninterested

overeating/loss of appetite

anxiety

feel can't cope

drug dependency

drinking/smoking more

### in children

going back to bad habits

illness: headaches, tummyaches

being defiant, shouting

angry, aggressive, violent, grumpy

nail-biting, thumb-sucking

worse school reports

waking at night, nightmares

loss of appetite

toilet problems

stealing, lying

often tired

often bored

crying a lot

more squabbling

# Signposts (on the right track)

getting on better

listening to each other better

feeling valued

being praised

children fighting less

parents fighting less

children doing better at school

self-nurturing

not feeling guilty praising

receiving praise comfortably

enjoying spending time together

picnics and other pleasant outings

happy family mealtimes

laughter and fun

feeling cheerful

acknowledging and expressing feelings clearly and safely

making new friends

finding life less stressful

more energy

positive attitude

problems solved more easily

feeling confident about the children

# Major Hazards

## (Extra-stressful situations)

death of someone close

divorce, new partner, remarriage

moving house

changing school, changing job

growing older – children and adults

friends moving away

redundancy

bullying/being bullied

financial worries

illness

breakdown in important friendships

peer pressure

exams

parental pressure

elderly parents

# In Case of Breakdown

## (Emergency survival kit)

find The Parenting Puzzle

think about the problem: problem-solve

talk to a friend

listen to others

ask for help, from friends, family, agencies, school, GP, counsellor, social services

set aside time to think about where the family is going

think before acting

put myself in the children's shoes

ask someone else to look after the family for a day or two, and take a break

There are times when life is tough. These are often the times when being a parent is difficult, too. If we plan ahead by thinking of ways to help us through the hard times, we may feel more able to cope when they happen.

Think of five things to help you look after your own needs when you are feeling down, and five more things you could do to help you as a parent when you are struggling. Use your own ideas, and refer to the list on page 243 as well if you would like to. Remember – this list is here for you to look at on a bad day.

# Practice Sheet
## Emergency Survival Kit

My personal survival kit:

1 ..........................................................................................

2 ..........................................................................................

3 ..........................................................................................

4 ..........................................................................................

5 ..........................................................................................

My emergency parenting kit:

1 ..........................................................................................

2 ..........................................................................................

3 ..........................................................................................

4 ..........................................................................................

5 ..........................................................................................

# A Pat on the Back

Last but not least, we suggest you think of five things about yourself that you like. You could write them in along the fingers and thumb on this hand.

Then give yourself a big pat on the back!

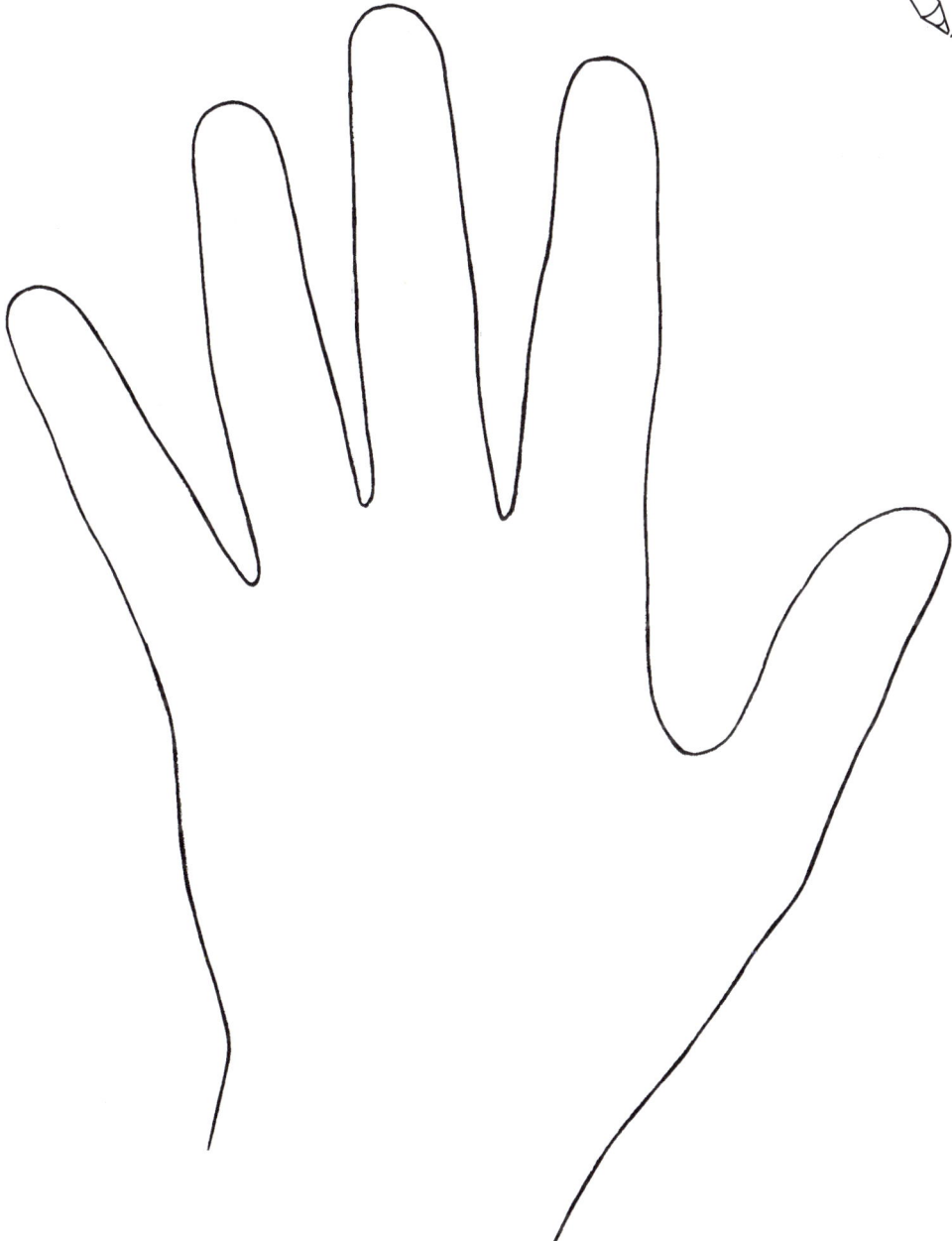

# REFLECTIONS

We're enjoying family life so much more than we used to! I'm feeling happier not only in myself and with the kids, but with my partner too.

Parenting is so much easier this way – I'm determined to hold on to all we have learnt.

The Programme has really helped me think about what I'd like to do differently for my children but I'm not sure I can do it yet. I wish I could do the course again.

It's been great to make friends, and to share problems and learn new ideas. I'd like to stay in touch.

I can see it would make a difference, but I'm finding it hard to change.

Most people have mixed feelings when we get to the end of the Programme. There's a sense of achievement, and it can also feel strange to think that we're not going to be meeting next week – we always wish we could spend more time together. Some parents like to go on meeting from time to time to give each other support. Others keep the time we've held the session as time to nurture themselves, and give themselves a weekly treat.

And of course it doesn't all end here. This is really another beginning, because there's the rest of our time as parents to go on putting all we've learnt into practice. We'll all slip back into old ways from time to time – it would be unreasonable to expect ourselves not to – but with a bit of luck we'll catch ourselves doing it, and pause to think about what we could do about it. Your Nurturing Toolbox is always there for you!

# REFLECTIONS

**? What are you thinking and feeling now we've come to the end of the course? If you would like to, record your own ideas here.**

................................................................

................................................................

................................................................

................................................................

# Time to Have a Go

SUN MON TUES WED THURS FRI SAT SUN MON TUES WED THURS FRI SAT

When you feel like it, it's useful to go back over the Time to Have a Go suggestions for all the previous sessions, and check what you are already doing. Pat yourself on the back!

You could then choose to focus on one extra idea, and when that is working well, move on to another one. Or you could use the ideas to help you think about something that is still a problem in the family, and decide what to try that might help.

Sometimes we feel like taking a break from trying anything new, and that is fine as well.

# well done!

you got to the end of the book
and the beginning of the next
stage in your family journey.

THE CENTRE FOR
**EMOTIONAL
HEALTH**

# CERTIFICATE

## * CONGRATULATIONS *

on completing

The Nurturing Programme

The centre for Emotional Health
wishes you all the best
for the future

# Books to Read

For those of you who enjoy reading, there is a huge range of books to choose from. Many bookshops stock a good selection, and they are also available via online retailers. *From among the many books on parenting and related issues we have selected just a few that explore in more depth some of the major topics covered by The Nurturing Programme:*

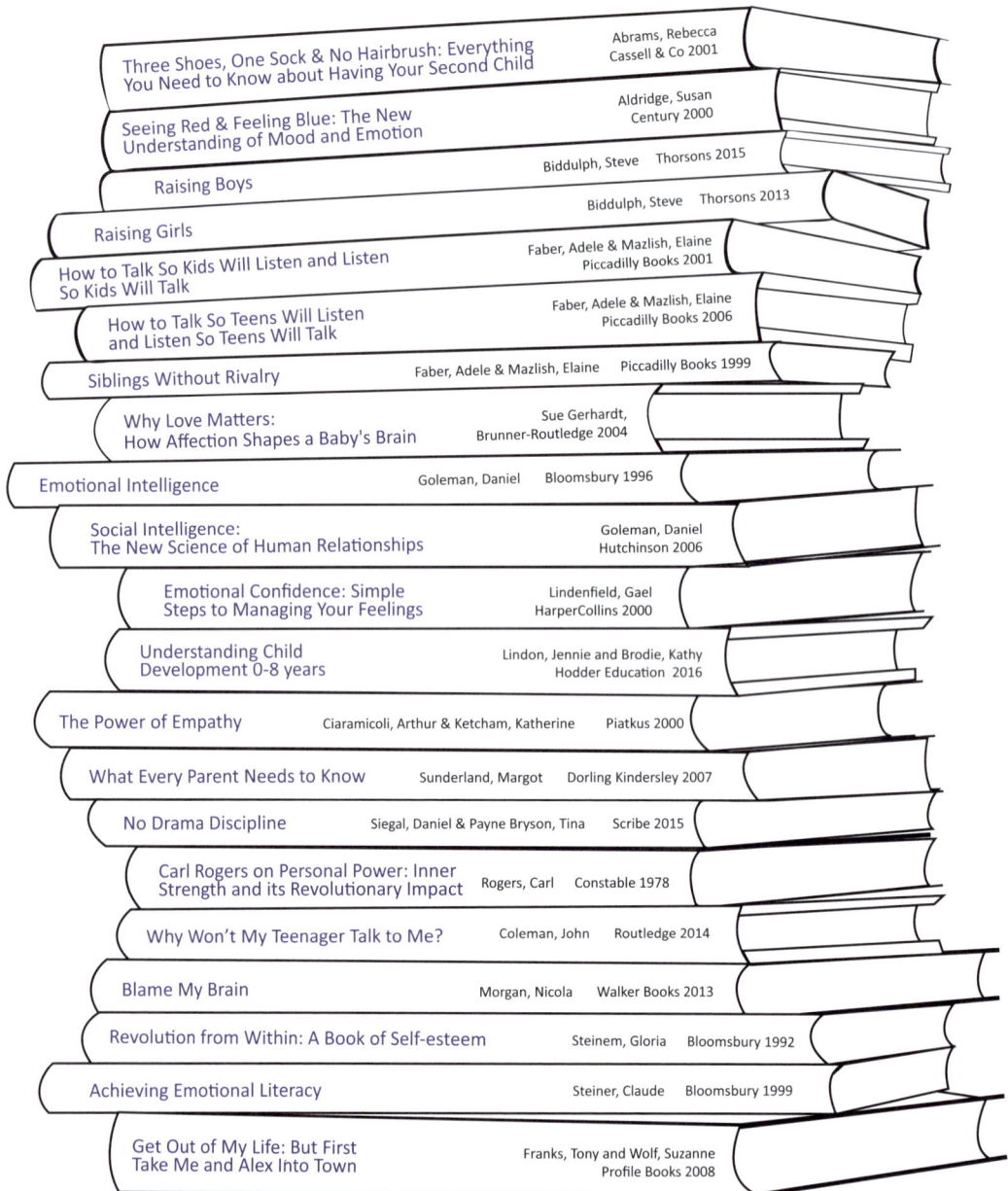

Three Shoes, One Sock & No Hairbrush: Everything You Need to Know about Having Your Second Child — Abrams, Rebecca — Cassell & Co 2001

Seeing Red & Feeling Blue: The New Understanding of Mood and Emotion — Aldridge, Susan — Century 2000

Raising Boys — Biddulph, Steve — Thorsons 2015

Raising Girls — Biddulph, Steve — Thorsons 2013

How to Talk So Kids Will Listen and Listen So Kids Will Talk — Faber, Adele & Mazlish, Elaine — Piccadilly Books 2001

How to Talk So Teens Will Listen and Listen So Teens Will Talk — Faber, Adele & Mazlish, Elaine — Piccadilly Books 2006

Siblings Without Rivalry — Faber, Adele & Mazlish, Elaine — Piccadilly Books 1999

Why Love Matters: How Affection Shapes a Baby's Brain — Sue Gerhardt, Brunner-Routledge 2004

Emotional Intelligence — Goleman, Daniel — Bloomsbury 1996

Social Intelligence: The New Science of Human Relationships — Goleman, Daniel — Hutchinson 2006

Emotional Confidence: Simple Steps to Managing Your Feelings — Lindenfield, Gael — HarperCollins 2000

Understanding Child Development 0-8 years — Lindon, Jennie and Brodie, Kathy — Hodder Education 2016

The Power of Empathy — Ciaramicoli, Arthur & Ketcham, Katherine — Piatkus 2000

What Every Parent Needs to Know — Sunderland, Margot — Dorling Kindersley 2007

No Drama Discipline — Siegal, Daniel & Payne Bryson, Tina — Scribe 2015

Carl Rogers on Personal Power: Inner Strength and its Revolutionary Impact — Rogers, Carl — Constable 1978

Why Won't My Teenager Talk to Me? — Coleman, John — Routledge 2014

Blame My Brain — Morgan, Nicola — Walker Books 2013

Revolution from Within: A Book of Self-esteem — Steinem, Gloria — Bloomsbury 1992

Achieving Emotional Literacy — Steiner, Claude — Bloomsbury 1999

Get Out of My Life: But First Take Me and Alex Into Town — Franks, Tony and Wolf, Suzanne — Profile Books 2008

# Books to read with children

**It is even harder to offer a selection from the hundreds of children's books available.**

*Here are some of our favourites to help children explore their feelings:*

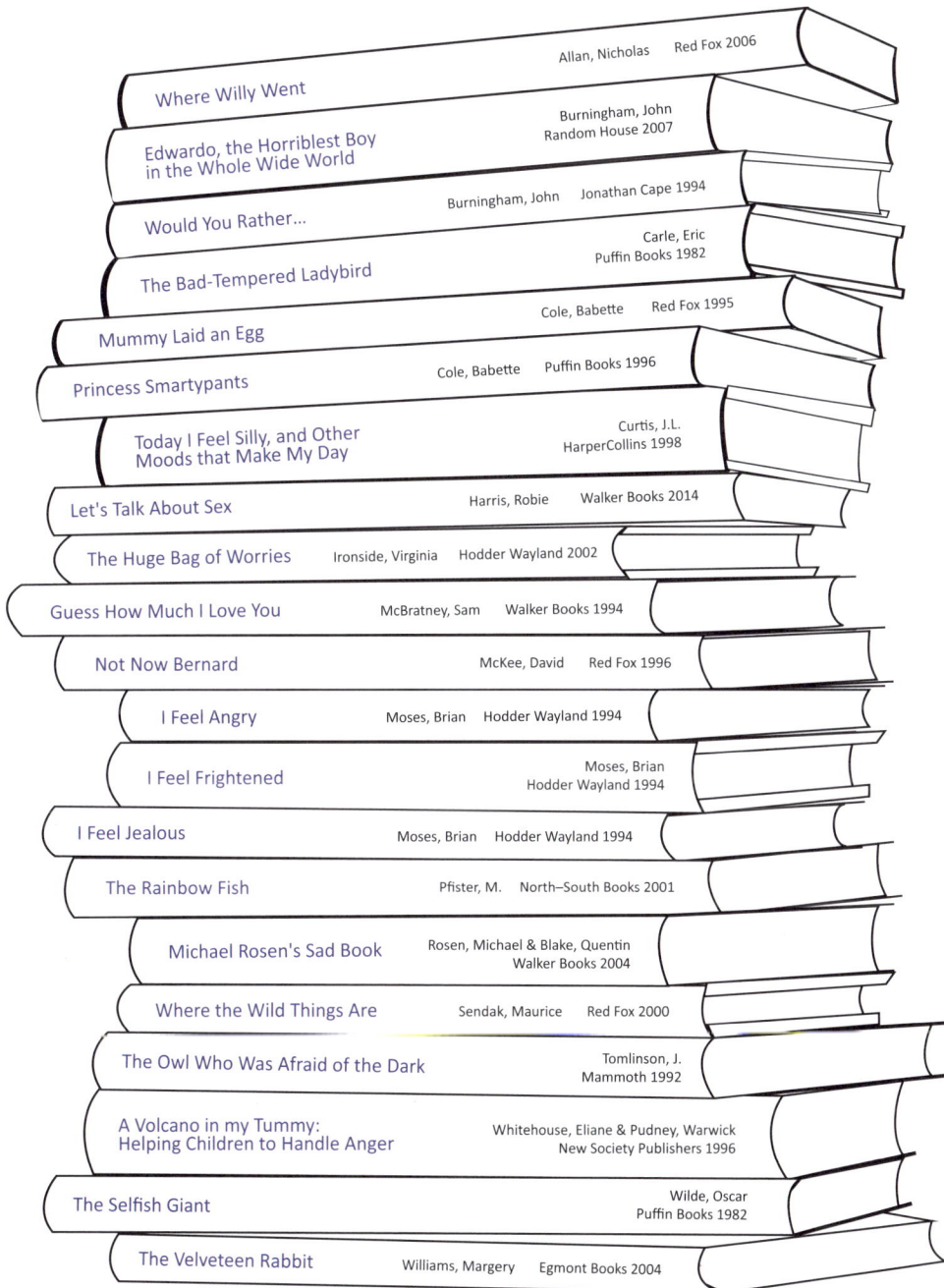

| Title | Author | Publisher |
|---|---|---|
| Where Willy Went | Allan, Nicholas | Red Fox 2006 |
| Edwardo, the Horriblest Boy in the Whole Wide World | Burningham, John | Random House 2007 |
| Would You Rather... | Burningham, John | Jonathan Cape 1994 |
| The Bad-Tempered Ladybird | Carle, Eric | Puffin Books 1982 |
| Mummy Laid an Egg | Cole, Babette | Red Fox 1995 |
| Princess Smartypants | Cole, Babette | Puffin Books 1996 |
| Today I Feel Silly, and Other Moods that Make My Day | Curtis, J.L. | HarperCollins 1998 |
| Let's Talk About Sex | Harris, Robie | Walker Books 2014 |
| The Huge Bag of Worries | Ironside, Virginia | Hodder Wayland 2002 |
| Guess How Much I Love You | McBratney, Sam | Walker Books 1994 |
| Not Now Bernard | McKee, David | Red Fox 1996 |
| I Feel Angry | Moses, Brian | Hodder Wayland 1994 |
| I Feel Frightened | Moses, Brian | Hodder Wayland 1994 |
| I Feel Jealous | Moses, Brian | Hodder Wayland 1994 |
| The Rainbow Fish | Pfister, M. | North–South Books 2001 |
| Michael Rosen's Sad Book | Rosen, Michael & Blake, Quentin | Walker Books 2004 |
| Where the Wild Things Are | Sendak, Maurice | Red Fox 2000 |
| The Owl Who Was Afraid of the Dark | Tomlinson, J. | Mammoth 1992 |
| A Volcano in my Tummy: Helping Children to Handle Anger | Whitehouse, Eliane & Pudney, Warwick | New Society Publishers 1996 |
| The Selfish Giant | Wilde, Oscar | Puffin Books 1982 |
| The Velveteen Rabbit | Williams, Margery | Egmont Books 2004 |

# Index

match what we expect with what they can do

playing helps children learn

what we pay attention to is what we get more of

gentle touch is loving touch

be assertive - use "I" statements

we all have power - our personal power

empathy is your ace card

children need to be told about sex

empathy helps people to feel understood

unwelcome touch is "ugh-ugh" touch

all labels are limiting

time to calm down works best when parents are calm too

let's solve problems not fight about them

clear fair rules help us all feel safe

giving choices makes children responsible

having fun boosts self esteem

the longest journey begins with the first step

praise is magic

feelings are signposts

what we pay attention to is what we get more of

we're on the lookout for kindness

nurturing ourselves SPICES up our lives

DOS work better than DON'TS

if we always do what we've always done, we'll always get what we've always got